CONTENTS

Guide for lottery astrologers:

A victory for all stars

Introduction:

Welcome to the Lottery Astrologer's Guide, where the power of astrology meets the thrill of winning the lottery.
On this fascinating and transformative journey, we will delve into the ancient wisdom of Hermesianism and trace its origins back to the mysterious emerald tablet of Hermes Trismegistos. In this mysterious area, the phrase "as above, as follows" has a deep meaning.
Using this guide as a compass, you'll begin a step-by-step exploration of how astrology reveals the secrets of predicting lottery winning numbers.

This book isn't just about winning a game of chance; It's about embracing the infinite possibilities within you. It is an invitation to explore your unique gifts and align them with the cosmic forces that shape our world.
Whatever your astrological experience or previous astrological experience, this guide welcomes you with open arms.

It aims to empower and inspire people from all walks of life, giving them the tools and knowledge to unleash their hidden potential and enrich themselves in all aspects of their lives.
As you turn the page, you will discover how the complex dance of stars and planets affects our daily lives and, most importantly, how you can use this celestial energy to your advantage.
It's not just a collection of general predictions or lucky numbers; It is a holistic approach to understanding the profound interactions between cosmic energy and our destiny.

So get ready for a journey that will change your life.
Embrace the power of astrology and the wisdom of time.
Let the guide of the lottery astrologer be your faithful companion, discover the secrets of the stars, pave the way to winning the

lottery, not only win the lottery, but live a fuller and richer life. It's time to free your inner lottery astrologer and create your own destiny. Welcome to your extraordinary adventure.

CHAPTER 1: PERSPECTIVES OF ASTROLOGY:

I.   Discover the mysteries of the universe behind lottery predictions.

It is an interesting world of astrology, where the celestial bodies and their movements have a deep understanding of the mysteries of life.

While astrology is not guaranteed to win numbers, it can provide a framework for understanding the cosmic energies that affect luck and happiness.

Astrology is an ancient practice that studies the position and movement of celestial bodies, applying the principle of "as above, as follows."

This suggests that patterns observed in the sky reflect patterns and events that occur on Earth.
By analyzing these celestial alignments, astrologers can gain a deeper understanding of all aspects of human existence, including the realms of luck and chance.

When it comes to lottery predictions, astrology offers a unique perspective when considering the cosmic effects at the time of the draw.

The key principle behind this approach is the belief that planetary positions and interactions can influence our lives and shape the energetic environment in which we live.

To understand the cosmic mysteries behind the lottery predictions, we first need to explore the concept of constellations and houses.
Each constellation represents a specific energy archetype, while houses represent different areas of life in which these energies manifest.

By analyzing horoscopes and families associated with good luck and abundance, astrologers can better understand the potential for lottery-friendly outcomes.

The planets also play an important role in lottery astrology.
Each planet has its own energy and symbolism that can influence our experiences and outcomes.
Jupiter, for example, known as the planet of expansion and luck, is often associated with favorable lottery outcomes.

Your position in the birth chart or at the time of the draw can provide valuable information about luck and possible odds of winning.

In addition, aspects of planet formation improve our understanding of lottery predictions.
These aspects represent geometric angles between the planets, indicating how their energies interact and influence each other.

Positive aspects, such as the third and sixties, indicate a harmonious energy and may indicate a favorable environment for the success of the lottery.
Weather is also a key factor in astrological lottery predictions.
By studying planetary transits, the movements of planets in relation to an individual's birth chart, astrologers can determine periods when cosmic energy promotes good luck and economic gain.

These shipping deadlines can serve as a potential time slot for entering the lottery.
While astrology provides a unique lens through which you can observe the influence of the universe on lottery results, it's important to look at it from a balanced perspective.
Lottery games are inherently random and no astrological knowledge can guarantee accurate winning numbers.

However, astrology can provide insight into the effects of energy on work and provide guidance for informed decision-making.

In short, we reveal the secrets of the universe behind lottery predictions through the lens of astrology.
By learning about constellations, houses, planets, aspects, and time, we can gain a deeper understanding of the energetic forces that shape our experiences of happiness and happiness.

While astrology is not a guarantee of a lottery's success, it can provide valuable information and a framework for making informed decisions.

Explore the connection between celestial bodies and potential happiness:

Welcome to the fascinating world of astrology, where the movement and position of celestial bodies is said to influence our lives and shape our destiny.
We'll look at the interesting connection between celestial bodies and potential luck and provide valuable insights into how you can use astrology to improve your understanding of the lottery.

Astrology is based on the basic principle that there is a profound interaction between the macroscopic world (the universe) and the microcosm (human existence).

The belief "as above, as follows" suggests that the patterns and energies observed in the sky are reflected in the patterns and energies of our daily lives.
By studying celestial bodies and their interactions, astrologers seek to unravel the hidden connections between the universe and our personal experiences of happiness and wealth.

One of the main components of astrology is the zodiac, a sky divided into twelve equal parts, each of which represents a specific constellation.

Each zodiac sign is associated with certain qualities, traits, and energies that affect every aspect of our lives, including happiness.

For example, fire signs
(Aries, Leo, Sagittarius) is often associated with boldness, enthusiasm, and luck, while Earth signs (Taurus, Virgo, Capricorn) are associated with practicality, stability, and financial abundance.

In addition to the signs of the zodiac, astrologers analyze the lottery or the positions and aspects of the planets at the birth of a person in order to obtain information about possible luck.

It is believed that each planet has its own energy and symbolism that can influence our experience.
Jupiter, for example, which is known as an expanding and abundant planet, is often associated with good luck and favorable outcomes.

It is placed on a specific horoscope or celestial event and can provide valuable clues about potential luck in the lottery.

The study of astrology also includes the concept of transit, which refers to the movement of the planets in relation to an individual's birth chart or current celestial events.

Public transportation is used to monitor ongoing impacts and energy changes that can affect our lives.

By analyzing transits of major planets such as Jupiter or Venus, astrologers can identify periods when luck and fortune may occur more frequently, and guide people to make informed decisions about participating in the lottery during these favorable cosmic alignments.

In addition, astrology studies the relationship between the planets through different aspects, that is, the geometric angles that are formed between them.
These aspects can be harmonious or difficult, indicating the ease or tension of the exchange of energy between the planets.

Favorable aspects, such as third and sixty, can indicate the flow of positive energy and increase the likelihood of achieving favorable results in areas related to happiness and abundance.
It is important to note that astrology is not a guaranteed way to accurately predict the outcome of the lottery.

Lottery games are designed to be random, and there is no astrological technique that can provide a clear winning number.
However, astrology can provide valuable information and provide a deeper understanding of the cosmic influences that surround

good luck and potentially favorable outcomes.

Finally, we examine the relationship between celestial bodies and potential happiness in the context of astrology.
Through the study of horoscopes, planetary positions, aspects, and transit, astrology provides a framework for understanding the energetic effects that can affect our experience of happiness and wealth.

While astrology is not a guarantee of a lottery success, it can serve as a valuable tool to improve our understanding and make informed decisions.

CHAPTER 2: DISCOVER THE ZODIAC SIGNS AND HOUSES THAT CAN INFLUENCE THE OUTCOME OF THE LOTTERY.

Zodiac Symbols and Their Meanings

Sign	Glyph	Symbol	Keywords
Aries			Fierce, forceful, courageous, impulsive
Taurus			Sensuous, peaceful, stable, obstinate
Gemini			Mental, communicative, perceptive, superficial
Cancer			Nurturing, emotional, intuitive, empathetic, moody
Leo			Kingly, expressive, self-confident, ego-centered
Virgo			Chaste, detail oriented, serving, perfectionistic
Libra			Balance, harmony, reconciling, indecisive
Scorpio			Intense, instinctual, sexual, secretive
Sagittarius			Friendly, open-minded, philosophical, imprudent
Capricorn			Practical, ambitious, masterful
Aquarius			Revolutionary, intensive, abstract, intelligent, unpredictable
Pisces			Selfless, mystical, compassionate, imaginative, sensitive

Tips and predictions for starting the lottery

Constellation:

1.   Zodiac signs are divided into 12 categories, each of which represents a different personality trait and trait. Some astrologers believe that some zodiac signs may be luckier than others in certain circumstances, including speculative activities such as gambling or lotteries. Here's a summary of the logo and related elements:

•   Fire signs (Aries, Leo, Sagittarius): Fire signs are often associated with enthusiasm, confidence, and risk-taking, which some believe can be a favorable trait for lottery success.

•   Earth sign (Taurus, Virgo, Capricorn): The earth sign is often seen as grounded, practical, and focused. You can approach the lottery with a methodical and discreet mentality, highlighting practical strategies.

•   Air signs (Gemini, Libra, Aquarius): Air signs are often associated with intelligence, adaptability, and social interaction. They can use their analytical skills to study lottery models or play group games with others.

•   Water signs (Cancer, Scorpio, Pisces): Water signs are often known for their intuition, sensitivity, and emotional depth. You can rely on their feelings or intuitions when choosing lottery numbers.

House:

2.   The Palace of Astrology represents different areas of life and can be associated with different themes. Some astrologers may analyze specific homes to explore the potential for financial gain or good luck. While interpretation may vary, here are some houses that are sometimes associated with lottery predictions:

•   2. House: The second house is usually associated with personal finances, material possessions and values. Some astrologers may analyze the location of the planets in this house to evaluate possible financial gains, including lottery prizes.

•   5th house: The 5th house is traditionally associated with creativity, self-expression, and speculation. Some astrologers may consider this house when dealing with things related to gambling, lotteries, and gambling.

The constellations and their characteristics:

Each zodiac sign has unique features that can give an idea of the lottery results.
Understanding these signs is important to uncover their effects on happiness and wealth.

Aries (March 21 - April 19):

Aries is a fire sign ruled by Mars that exudes vitality, passion, and competitiveness.
People born under this zodiac sign often have a strong desire for success, which can increase their luck in the lottery.
They thrive in situations where risk-taking and quick decisions are required.

Taurus (April 20 – May 20):

Taurus, the Earth sign ruled by Venus, represents stability and practicality.
People born under this zodiac sign tend to approach the lottery with a cautious and methodical mentality.
They can choose numbers associated with material abundance, or they can rely on their innate intuition.

Gemini (May 21 to June 20):

Gemini, the air sign ruled by Mercury, embodies versatility, adaptability, and intellectual abilities. People affected by this flag can use analytical strategies and mathematical calculations to choose their lottery numbers. In addition, the twins' penchant for communication and networking through group games or soap bubbles can lead to lottery success.

Cancer (June 21 - July 22):

Cancer, the water sign ruled by the Moon, represents emotional depth, intuition, and affection.
The predictions of the Cancer Lottery can be deeply rooted in your intuitive vision and sensitivity to energy.
These people may rely on dream interpretations, tarot cards, or other divination tools to guide the choice of numbers.

Leo (July 23 - August 22):

Leo is a fire sign ruled by the Sun and exudes confidence, creativity, and leadership.
Lottery predictions for Leo usually involve trusting his instincts and embracing his charismatic nature.
You may also prefer numbers associated with size, success, and self-expression.

Virgo (August 23 - September 22):

Virgo, the Earth sign ruled by Mercury, is synonymous with practicality, precision, and analysis.
Virgo approaches the lottery with meticulousness and attention to detail.
They can use statistical analysis, historical data, or models to increase their chances of success.

Libra (September 23 to October 22):

Libra is a sign ruled by Venus and personifies harmony, balance, and diplomacy.
Those affected by Libra can look for combinations of numbers that reflect symmetry or equilibrium. They can also benefit from partnership or group games, as their collaborative nature can

increase their chances of winning.

Scorpio (October 23 - November 21):

Scorpio, the water sign ruled by Pluto, represents strength, intuition, and transformation. Those born under this zodiac sign can use its intuitive power and immerse themselves in esoteric practices to predict lottery outcomes.
They can also promote numbers associated with secrets, hidden knowledge, and personal transformations.

Sagittarius (November 22 - December 21):

Sagittarius is a fire sign ruled by Jupiter that embodies adventure, optimism, and exploration. Sagittarians can rely on their general mindset and philosophical intuition to approach lottery predictions.
They may also appreciate numbers related to travel, education, or spiritual growth.

Capricorn (December 22 – January 19):

Capricorn, the Earth sign ruled by Saturn, represents ambition, discipline and structure. People influenced by Capricorn tend to approach the lottery with strategic thinking. They can count on convenience, analysis, and long-term planning when choosing their numbers. Capricorns can also choose numbers related to material success and stability.

Aquarius (January 20 to February 18):

Aquarius is the sign ruled by Uranus and personifies innovation, independence and intellectual activity.
Lottery predictions for Aquarius often involve thinking outside the box and using unconventional strategies.
You can choose numbers that relate to technological advancements or social trends. Aquarius can also experiment

with unique combinations of values or random selection methods.

Pisces (February 19 – March 20):

Pisces is the water sign ruled by Neptune, which means compassion, imagination, and spiritual connection.
People born under this zodiac sign can rely on their intuitive intuition and connection with the subconscious mind to predict lottery outcomes.
You can choose numbers associated with dreams, intuitions, or spiritual symbols.

The Palace of Astrology and its influences:

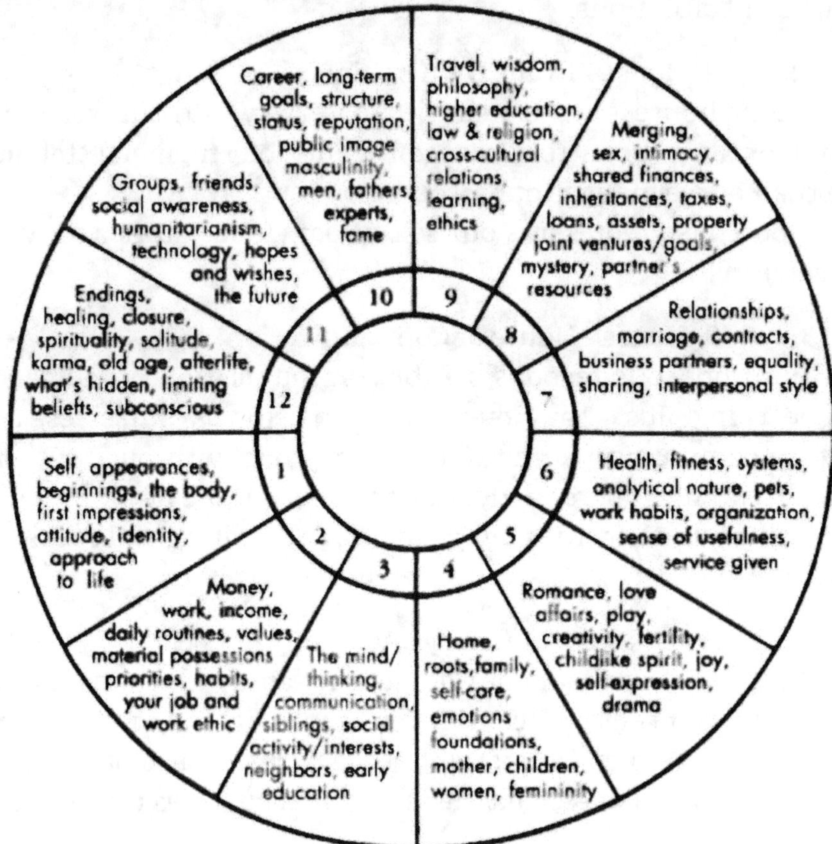

The 12 Houses of Astrology play an important role in understanding all aspects of our lives and the different areas they manage.

Each house represents a specific area of existence and has a unique meaning and influence.

In this chapter, we will examine the meaning of each of the 12 astrological palaces, their symbolic representations, and the area of life they govern.

1.   1. House - house of oneself:

The first house represents the self, the flesh, and the way we present ourselves to the world. It determines our personality, our appearance and our lifestyle in general. The house also talks about our sense of identity, our self-image and how we assert ourselves in different situations.

2.   2. House - Home Ownership:

The second house is associated with material wealth, finances and personal value. It controls our profitability, our financial stability and the way we manage our resources.

This house also represents our self-esteem, our values and what we value in life.

3.   3. House - House of Communication:

The third house is responsible for communication, intelligence and learning. It's about our ability to express ourselves, the way we communicate, and our relationships with our brothers and sisters, neighbors, and local communities. The house also represents our curiosity, mental agility, and writing and speaking skills.

4.   Fourth house - family and family house:

The 4th house represents our home, our family and our roots. It determines our sense of security, our emotional foundations, and our connection to our ancestral lineage. Home is also our private life, our family business and the nutritional qualities we embody.

5.   House 5 - House of Creativity and Romance:
The fifth house is associated with self-expression, creativity, romance and fun. Master our artistic talents, hobbies and activities that bring us joy. Home also represents our romantic relationships, our love, and how we seek recognition and recognition.

6.   House 6 - House of Health and Services:
The sixth house is associated with health, work and service to others. It determines our daily lives, our work ethic and the way we maintain our physical and mental health. The house also represents our attitude to service, organization and our ability to handle practical tasks.

7.   7. House - House of the Association:
House 7 represents personal and professional associations. It regulates our personal relationships, marriages and business partnerships. This House is also about our ability to work together, to compromise and to seek harmony in our relationships.

8.   House 8 - House of Transformation:
The 8th house is associated with transformation, resource sharing and deep connectedness. It regulates our privacy, our shared finances, and the mysteries of life and death. It also represents our ability to effect personal transformations and our attitude towards shared resources and power dynamics.

9.   House 9 - House of Expansion and Higher Education:
The ninth house stands for higher education, travel, philosophy and spirituality. It determines our pursuit of knowledge, belief and our search for meaning and purpose in life. Home is also associated with our sense of adventure, cultural exploration, and connection with higher truths and spiritual aspirations.

10.   House 10 - House of Occupation and Public Image:
The 10th house is associated with our profession, our social

status and our public image. It determines our ambitions, our achievements and our reputation in the public eye. This house also represents our career goals, authority figures, and contribution to society.

11.   House 11 - House of Friendship and Community:
The 11th house stands for friendship, social groups and our participation in the community. It dominates our network of friends, our social environment and our desire for community. This house is also our commitment to humanitarian causes, our ability to work with others, our hopes and dreams for the future.

12.   Twelfth House - House of Spirituality and the Inner World:
The twelfth house deals with the spiritual, unconscious, and hidden aspects of our mind. It determines our connection with the divine, our dreams, and the process of overcoming ourselves. Home also represents loneliness, introspection, and our ability to explore universal consciousness.

CHAPTER 3: PLANETARY MODELS:

Check the planetary alignment and its impact on lottery results:

Now, let's dive into the realm of planetary models and their profound impact on lottery results.

Remember the ancient hermetic principle of "as above, as below" as we explore the connection between heaven and lottery.

1. Planetary Dance:

A planetary model refers to the unique configuration of planetary formations at a given point in time.
These patterns have a significant impact on the energy and dynamics of the universe, which in turn affects our lives, including lottery results.
Let's dive into some important planetary models and their potential impact on lottery results.

1.   Connect:

A conjunction occurs when two planets are aligned in the same constellation or degree of the zodiac.

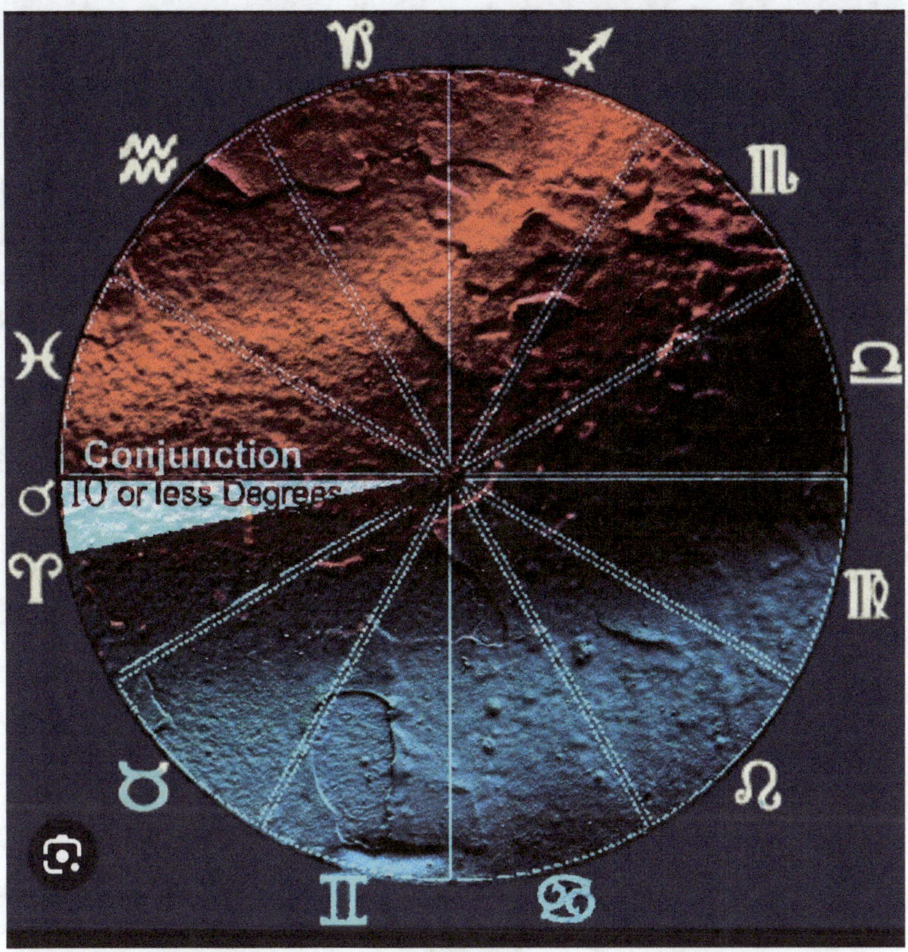

This alignment creates a powerful energy that can manifest itself in a variety of ways, including influencing lottery results.
The conjunction of useful planets such as Jupiter and Venus could mean more happiness and potential to make money.

On the other hand, conjunctions involving malevolent planets such as Saturn or Mars can indicate challenges or delays in achieving lottery success.

2.   Trigoni:

Experiments occur when the planets are about 120 degrees apart, forming a harmonious angle. Triplets represent a liquid energy that contributes to simple and positive results.

If the 3rd house coincides with the provisional position and finances, such as the 2nd or 5th house, favorable conditions for winning the lottery can be displayed.

Experiments involving beneficial planets such as Jupiter or Venus can increase the likelihood of financial gains and asset collapses.

3.   Square:

When planets are about 90 degrees apart, squares are formed, creating dynamic and difficult energy.

The square represents the tensions and obstacles that require effort and adaptation to be overcome. When squares are aligned with homes associated with luck and finances, they may indicate that caution must be exercised and lottery predictions must be carefully considered.

Blocks involving evil planets such as Saturn or Mars can mean delays, setbacks, or more competition to succeed in the lottery.

4.   Opposition:

Opposition occurs when planets are about 180 degrees apart, creating balanced, polarized energy.

Opposition is a conflict between opposing forces that needs to be reconciled. If objections coincide with luck and financial budgets, they may indicate that a balance must be struck between risk-taking and caution in lottery activities. Opposition with useful planets can bring unexpected reward opportunities, while opposition with evil planets can present challenges or obstacles to winning the lottery.

II. Using Planetary Models in Lottery Predictions:

Understanding planetary patterns is only the first step. The key is to incorporate this knowledge into your lottery predictions.
Here are some ways to use planetary models to look for accurate and detailed lottery predictions:

1.   Planetary Transus

A transit occurs when a planet passes between a star and its observers.
Since Venus or Mercury travel between us and the Sun, transits in the solar system can be observed from Earth.

Pay attention to the current transits of the planet and how they interact with your horoscope or a horoscope of important events, such as.dem the start of a lottery draw.

A transit of useful planets such as Jupiter or Venus could mean more luck and potential gains, while transits of malevolent planets may require more caution or a strategic approach.

2.   Calculation of time:

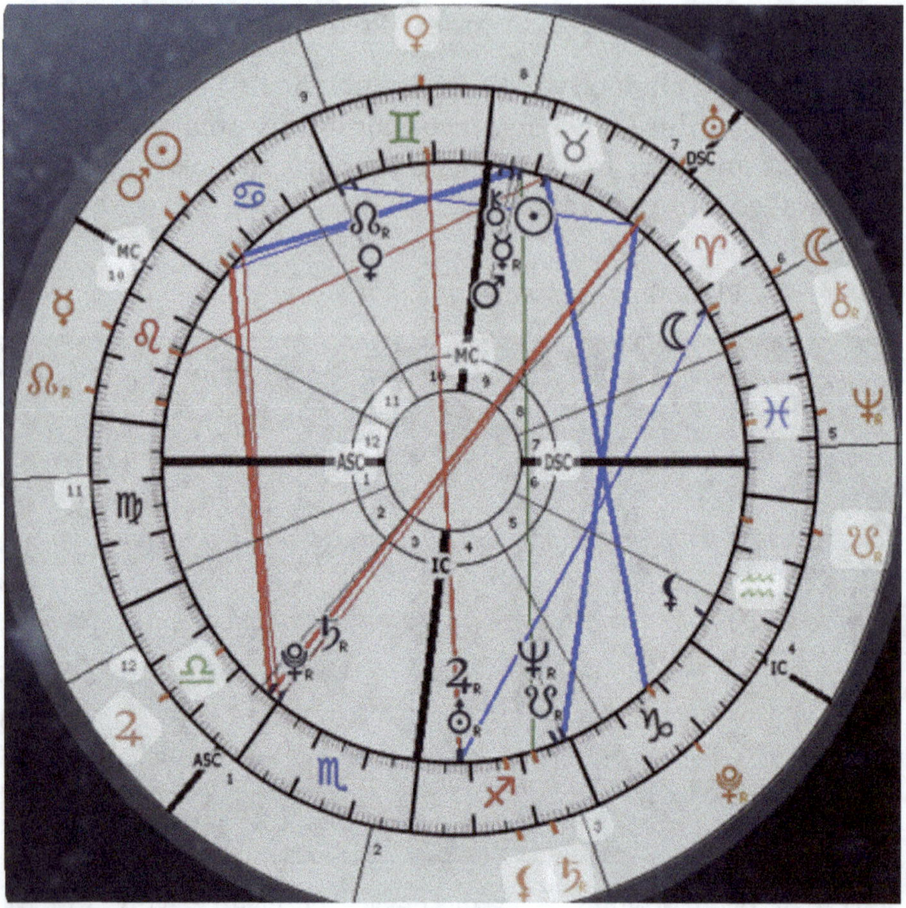

Think of planetary models with big lottery draws or when tickets have been purchased.

For example, if the favorable conjunction or 3rd house coincides with the 5th house or the date of the draw, it could indicate that it is a good time to play and increase your chances of success.

3.   Personal birth card:

Analyze your birth chart or the birth chart of the person participating in the lottery.

It identifies all significant planetary patterns and their correspondence with families related to happiness and finance.
Look for models that have great potential for lottery success, such as advantageous planets in key locations or harmonious aspects between planets.
This information can help you choose numbers and help you make an informed decision.

4.	Astrology Software and Resources:

Use astrology software or consult professional astrologers who specialize in financial astrology or lottery forecasting.
These features can provide detailed information about planetary models and their impact on lottery results.
You can create custom reports, calculate favorable dates and times, and provide expert advice based on the birth chart and specific situation.

5.	Intuition and awareness:

Trust your instincts and watch over the energy of the universe.
While astrology provides a structured framework for predicting lottery outcomes, it's important to listen to your inner voice and be aware of any intuitive drives or synchronicities that might lead you to the right numbers or opportunities.

CHAPTER 4: UNRAVELING THE MYSTERIES OF HUMILIATION, CONJUNCTION AND TRANSGRESSION

During our journey through the cosmic realm of astrology and its connection to lottery predictions, we explore the influence of astrological signs, houses, and planetary patterns.
Now let's look at three important celestial phenomena, namely: Retrograde, conjunction and transit

By understanding the complexity of these celestial events, we gain valuable insights into the dynamics of the universe and how they affect lottery results.
Now, let's unravel the mystery and use retrograde power, conjunction and transit to accurately predict the lottery.

1.   Retrograde: the dance of cosmic rewinding

Retrograde occurs when a planet appears to move away from Earth's perspective in its orbit.
This apparent backward movement brings with it unique energy and influence that can affect lottery predictions.
Let's explore some of the key bearish grades and their potential impact:

First, Mercury retrograde:
Mercury retrograde is probably the most well-known retrograde associated with communication failures, technical failures, and delays.
During this time, it is advisable to check the lottery numbers, carefully communicate and negotiate, and prepare for unexpected twists and turns. However, not every Mercury retrograde is negative, and with proper awareness and preparation, it is possible to navigate effectively during this period.

Secondly, Venus retrograde:
Venus retrograde gives us the opportunity to reflect and re-evaluate your values, relationships, and financial issues.
When it comes to lottery predictions, this may be the right time to rethink your strategy, rethink your digital options, and focus on wealth from within.
Use this time to deepen your intuition and align your desires with your actions.

Third, Mars retrograde:
Mars retrograde causes a shift in energy, highlighting the need for introspection, patience and caution.
Now is the time to re-evaluate your motivations, actions, and desires. When it comes to lottery predictions, it may be wise to exercise moderation and avoid impulsive decisions. Instead, focus on strategy, refine your approach, and align your business with your long-term goals.

2.   Conjunction: Celestial Alliance and Mighty Energy

Conjunction occurs when two or more planets in the same constellation or stage are aligned in the zodiac, mixing their energies and creating a powerful force that can affect the outcome of the lottery.

Let's explore the meaning of conjunction words in lottery predictions:

1. The conjunction of Jupiter and Venus:

Jupiter and Venus are known as useful planets associated with good luck, abundance, and prosperity. When the two planets form a conjunction, it increases the potential for economic gains, including lottery prizes. This alignment implies a favorable period of time to participate in the lottery, choose numbers that are relevant to wealth, and trust your instincts.

2. Sun-Moon Connection:

The conjunction of the Sun and Moon, also known as the New Moon, represents a new beginning, a new beginning, and greater intuition. This is the perfect time to set intentions, imagine success, and focus your energy on the desired outcome. During this bond, consider choosing lottery numbers that match your intentions and your heart's desires.

Third, the conjunction of the outer planets:

Conjunctions involving exoplanets such as Saturn, Uranus, Neptune, and Pluto carry transformative energies that can influence lottery predictions.

These alignments often indicate significant changes, challenges, or unforeseen opportunities. Notice the area of life that these planets dominate in their natal chart and how their conjunctions coincide with the locations of homes associated with happiness and finances.

Adjust your strategy accordingly and be open to opportunities.

3.   Transit: Celestial Journey and Time

A transit refers to the movement of a planet that passes through different constellations of the zodiac and aligns with a specific point in the horoscope or an important event such as a tie. Understanding planetary transits is essential to get accurate lottery predictions. Let's explore what it means:

I. Personal transport:
Keep an eye out for transits of the planets, as they make up all aspects of your natal chart.
When planets like Jupiter, Venus, or the Sun form aspects that harmonize with your birth chart, it is related to luck and finances and suggests favorable times for lottery predictions.
Use this time to play with confidence, trust your instincts and choose numbers that match the positive energy of these transiting planets.

2. Lunar transit:
A lunar transit can have a profound impact on our emotions, intuitions, and instincts.
Note the position of the moon in the natal chart, as well as its daily movement as it forms phases with other planets.
During the full and new moons, the moon has a particularly large influence on lottery results, and high energy can increase your chances of success.

3. Exoplanet transit:
Transits of exoplanets such as Saturn, Uranus, Neptune and Pluto often signify a time of change in our lives.
If these planets are associated with happiness and finances in terms of starting a family, it may indicate a significant change in your finances or an unexpected chance of winning the lottery.
Get to know the lessons learned and the growth potential of this transport and adjust your lottery strategy accordingly.

4. Harnessing the power of degradation, conjunction and transit

To effectively use degradation, conjunction and transit in lottery predictions, you should consider the following:

1. History:
Beware of mishaps, conjunctions, and transit moments related to draws or buying lottery tickets.
Plan your engagement during favorable alignment phases to maximize your chances of success.

II. Understanding and preparation:
Stay up to date on major deteriorations, conjunctions, and upcoming transits.
Use this knowledge to address potential challenges, refine your strategy, and align with the positive energy available during these celestial events.

3. Self-reflection and intuition:
Demotion, conjunction and transit offer opportunities for self-reflection,
Introspective and sharp intuition. Use this time to dive into your inner wisdom, trust your instincts, and adjust your lottery predictions based on the advice you receive.

5.   Practical guide:
Conjunctions occur when two or more planets with the same constellation or degree align in the zodiac and mix their energies.
The transit provides valuable information about the weather, which allows us to align our strategy with the cosmic current.
By incorporating the wisdom of degradation, conjunction and transit into our lottery predictions, we improve our ability to accurately predict outcomes.

CHAPTER 5: IDENTIFYING PLANETARY CONFIGURATIONS FOR LOTTERY SUCCESS

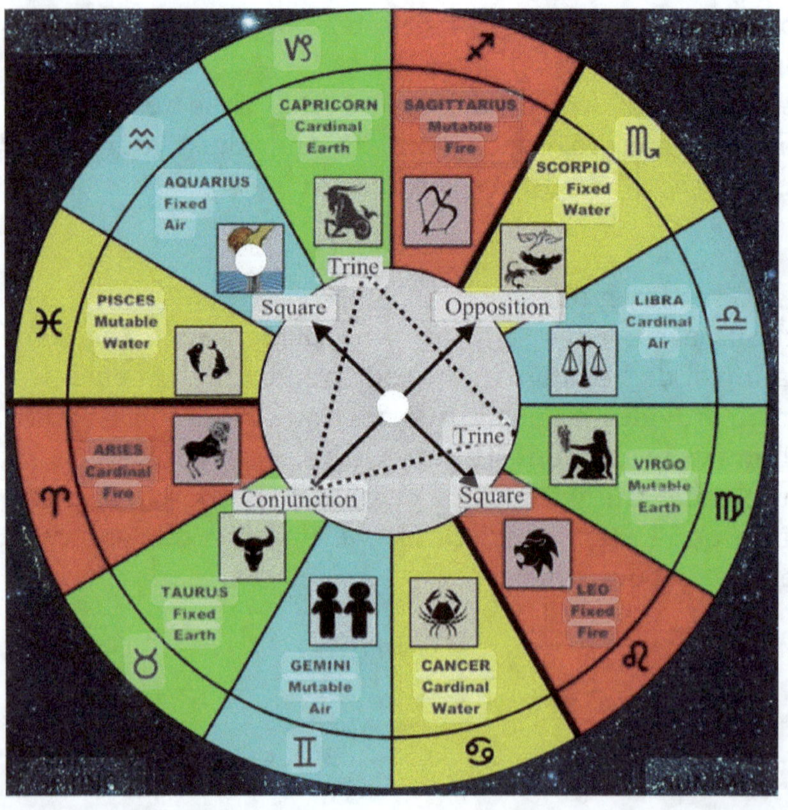

1.   **The Great Solar Trigon:**

The Great Trident is a powerful configuration that occurs when three planets form equilateral triangles on a natal or transit horoscope.

This configuration represents a harmonious energy and flow between the planets involved. If a large 3rd house matches a house associated with good luck, such as .dem 2nd or 5th house, it indicates a higher probability of success in the lottery.

Pay attention to the elements involved (fire, earth, air, or water) and choose numbers that match those elements to increase your chances.

2.   **Mysterious rectangle:**

The mysterious rectangle is a unique configuration of two opposites and two sextants that form a rectangular shape on a natal chart or transit map.

This configuration combines the energy of challenge and opportunity.

When a mysterious rectangle is associated with a home associated with happiness and finances, it suggests a moment of balance and achievement.

This means that hard work, strategy, and seizing opportunities can lead to successful lottery periods.

Make a note of the planets involved and the corresponding numbers to determine your choice of numbers.

3.   **Yode (Finger of Fate):**

Yod, also known as the "Finger of Fate," is a rare and important constellation that occurs when two planets form a quartile and both are third planets.

This formation resembles a long, narrow triangle pointing to a specific area of a horoscope or traffic map.

When Yod connects to a house associated with good luck, he represents a strong cosmic sign of the potential success of the lottery.

The key is to pay attention to the planets on Yod and the energies they represent. Choose numbers for your lottery predictions that match the quality and theme of the planet.

4.   Star:

A constellation is when three or more planets are grouped in the same constellation or near a house.

This configuration involves a focus on the energy and intensity of a particular area of life.

If the zodiac sign coincides with families related to luck and finances, it suggests that this is a time of great potential for financial gain, including lottery prizes.

Study the planets involved and the corresponding numbers to make the choice of number.

Think about the characteristics and arguments that have to do with the zodiac sign.

5.   Saturn-Jupiter conjunction:

The conjunction of Saturn with Jupiter is a major celestial event that occurs about once every 20 years.

This means that the confluence of expansion (Jupiter) and structure (Saturn) creates a powerful combination of happiness and stability.

When this combination is balanced with happiness and financially connected families, it heralds a time of great potential for financial growth and success.

This alignment implies an opportune time to participate in the draw, and the numbers chosen reflect both the expansionist qualities of Jupiter and the disciplined approach of Saturn.

6.   Sun-Moon-Midsky Alignment:

The intermediate Sun-Moon-Sky alignment is important in astrology because it represents the essence (Sun), the emotional landscape (Moon) and the public call (center of the sky). When these three elements are associated with families related to happiness and finances, it indicates a moment of alignment with your true self, emotional clarity, and possible public recognition.

This setup involves more insight and self-awareness, which can greatly improve lottery predictions.

Trust your instincts and choose numbers that align with your true self and desire for financial success.

7.   For the good of the planet:

Pay attention to the transits of the favored planets, such as Jupiter and Venus, as they are favorable for the location of the house, which is associated with luck and financial situation in the birth chart or transit map.

These crossings include periods of greater happiness, abundance, and economic gain potential. Align your lottery efforts with these crossovers to maximize your chances of success.

Choose numbers that reflect the mass and energy associated with these planets to select numbers.

8.   Custom settings:

Finally, pay attention to any custom settings in the birth chart that might indicate a good time to win the lottery. Consult with a professional astrologer who can analyze your astrolabe and determine your specific planetary configuration. You can provide personalized information and tips for your lottery predictions so that you can take advantage of your astrological advantage.

9.   Practical guide:

Identify favorable planetary configurations that you can use as a powerful tool to increase your chances of success in the lottery.

The Great Trinity, mysterious rectangles, Yod, constellations, Saturn-Jupiter conjunctions, the average Sun-Moon-sky orientation, and advantageous planetary transits have great economic profit potential.

Learn, understand and tune in with these celestial environments, you will be able to make informed decisions and choose numbers that resonate with the energy of the game.

Remember to always combine your astrological knowledge with your intuition and personal strategies to optimize your lottery predictions.

CHAPTER 6: SIGNS OF THE ZODIAC

I. Immerse yourself in the signs of the zodiac and their relationship to happiness and wealth.

Aries (March 21 - April 19):
Aries is the fire sign of Mars' dominance and personifies ambition, confidence, and courage.
People born under this zodiac sign usually have a fighting spirit and a fearless attitude to challenges.
When it comes to the lottery, Aries can thrive in high-risk

situations and may be inclined to choose numbers associated with its lucky colors, such as bright red or fiery orange.

Taurus (April 20 – May 20):
Taurus, the Earth sign ruled by Venus, represents stability, expediency, and determination.
Taurus individuals tend to approach the lottery with a methodical, low-key mindset.
You may appreciate numbers that reflect the richness and stability of the material, or numbers associated with lucky stones such as emeralds or jade.

Gemini (May 21 to June 20):
Gemini, the air sign ruled by Mercury, embodies versatility, adaptability, and intellectual abilities. People born in this zodiac sign can use analytical strategies and mathematical calculations in their lottery predictions.
You may also be attracted to numbers associated with communication, duality, or happy days of the week like Wednesday.

Cancer (June 21 - July 22):
Cancer, the water sign ruled by the Moon, represents sensitivity, intuition and emotional depth. People born under this zodiac sign can rely on their intuition and intuitive intuition to predict their lottery predictions.
They may be attracted to numbers related to growth, family, or lucky numbers that have sentimental value.

Leo (July 23 - August 22):
Leo is a fire sign ruled by the Sun and exudes confidence, creativity, and leadership. Lions generally have strong confidence and optimism, which can affect their lottery predictions.
They tend to choose numbers related to size, success, or their lucky numbers, which are usually tied to their date of birth.

Virgo (August 23 - September 22):
Virgo, the Earth sign ruled by Mercury, is synonymous with

practicality, precision, and analysis.

Virgo tends to approach the lottery with meticulousness and attention to detail. You can use statistical analysis, historical data, or models when selecting numbers. Virgo can also be attracted to numbers associated with orders, services, or lucky colors such as navy blue or earth brown.

Libra (September 23 to October 22):

Libra is a sign ruled by Venus and personifies harmony, balance, and diplomacy.

Libra can look for combinations of values that reflect symmetry or balance in its lottery predictions.

They can also benefit from partnership or group games, as their collaborative nature can increase their chances of winning.

Numbers related to beauty, love, or your lucky number, which are often associated with the number 6, can also have meaning for people in Libra.

Scorpio (October 23 - November 21):

Scorpio, the water sign ruled by Pluto, represents intensity, intuition, and transformation. Those born in this zodiac sign can use their intuitive power to immerse themselves in esoteric practice and make lottery predictions.

Scorpios can be attracted to numbers associated with secrets, hidden knowledge, and personal transformations.

They can also be influenced by lucky numbers, which are often associated with the number 9, or combinations with deep personal meaning.

Sagittarius (November 22 - December 21):

Sagittarius is a fire sign ruled by Jupiter that personifies adventure, optimism, and expansion. If you are affected by this sign, you can approach the lottery with an overview and believe in your luck.

They may be drawn to numbers that have to do with travel, education, or lucky numbers, which are often associated with the number 3 or a combination that reflects their adventurous nature.

Capricorn (December 22 – January 19):
Capricorn, the Earth sign ruled by Saturn, represents ambition, discipline and structure. Capricorns approach the lottery with strategic thinking and focus on long-term planning. They tend to choose numbers that refer to material success, stability, or lucky numbers that correspond to their date of birth or important milestones.

Aquarius (January 20 to February 18):
Aquarius is the sign ruled by Uranus and personifies innovation, independence and intellectual activity.
Aquarius-influenced people can use unconventional strategies and unique combinations of numbers in their lottery predictions. They can be attracted by numbers related to technological advancements, social trends, or lucky numbers with symbolic value.

Pisces (February 19 – March 20):
Pisces is the water sign ruled by Neptune, which means compassion, imagination, and spiritual connection.
People born under this zodiac sign can rely on their intuitive intuition and connection with the subconscious mind when making lottery predictions.
You may be attracted to numbers associated with dreams, intuition, or lucky numbers that have a spiritual meaning.

Practical guide:

Delve deeper into the signs of the zodiac and their relationship to luck and luck to gain valuable insights into optimizing lottery predictions.
By understanding the quality and energy of each logo, we can tailor our digital selection strategy accordingly.
Whether it's the ardent ambitions of Aries, the meticulous analysis of Virgo, or the intuitive flashes of Cancer, each zodiac sign offers a unique approach to the lottery.

Combine your astrological knowledge with the intuition, personal strategies, and other techniques explored in this book to improve your ability to accurately predict lottery outcomes.

2. Analyze the unique qualities of each logo and its potential impact on lottery results:

Aries (March 21 – April 19): Pioneer of Fire
Aries is the main fire sign that reigns on Mars, personifying courage, ambition and determination. As pioneers, the Aryans treated the lottery with a fierce competitive spirit.
They thrive by taking risks and making bold decisions.
Self-confidence and courage can lead to positive results.
Aryans may be attracted to numbers that reflect their pioneering character, such as 1 or a combination that exudes energy and vitality.

Taurus (April 20 – May 20): A Realistic Statement

Taurus, a solid earth sign ruled by Venus, represents stability, expediency, and material abundance.
Taurus approaches the lottery with a solid and methodical mentality.
They rely on your patience and perseverance to express their desires.
Taurus may prefer wealth-related numbers such as 4s or combinations that reflect their love of beauty and luxury.

Gemini (May 21 – June 20): analytical communicator
Gemini is an ever-changing air sign ruled by Mercury and embodies versatility, curiosity, and intellectual ability.
Geminis approach the lottery with their analytical skills, using logical strategies and calculations.
They like to explore patterns and make informed decisions.

Geminis can be attracted to numbers related to communication and intelligence, such as 5 or combinations that reflect their dual nature.

Cancer (June 21 to July 22): the Nurifer intuition
Cancer, the water sign ruled by the Moon, represents sensitivity, empathy, and emotional depth.
People with cancer approach the lottery with intuition and emotional intelligence.
They trust their instincts and their connection to the subconscious mind. Cancer can be attracted to numbers related to parenting and family, such as 2 or a combination with sentimental value.

Leo (July 23 – August 22): Royal Artist
Leo is a firm fire sign ruled by the Sun that exudes confidence, creativity, and leadership. Lions approach the lottery with size and talent.
They believe in luck and shine when self-expression is required.
Leos may prefer numbers associated with success and self-realization, such as 9 or a combination that reflects their courageous and charismatic nature.

Virgo (August 23 – September 22): Meticulous Analyst
Virgo, an ever-changing Earth sign ruled by Mercury, represents practical, precise, and analytical thinking.
Virgo approaches the lottery with meticulousness and attention to detail.
They use statistical analysis, historical data, and pattern recognition to make informed decisions.
Virgo tends to choose numbers that relate to order and organization, such as 6 or combinations that reflect their attention to detail.

Libra (September 23 to October 22):
Harmonious diplomats
Libra is the cardinal sign ruled by Venus and embodies balance, harmony, and diplomacy. Libra approaches the lottery with a thirst for justice and cooperation.
They thrive when it comes to partnerships or group games. Libra can be attracted by numbers associated with beauty and love, such as 7.
Or a combination that reflects his love of symmetry and aesthetics.

Scorpio (October 23 - November 21): Strong Transformers
Scorpio, the solid water sign ruled by Pluto, represents intensity, passion, and transformation. Scorpios approach the lottery with their deep insight and inclination to discover hidden truths.
They are not afraid to take risks and immerse themselves in esoteric practices in order to increase the odds. Scorpios may be attracted to numbers associated with mystery and power, such as 8s or combinations with deep personal meaning.

Sagittarius (Nov. 22 - Dec. 21): Adventurous Optimist
Sagittarius is an ever-changing fire sign ruled by Jupiter and embodies adventure, optimism, and expansion. Sagittarians approach the lottery with enthusiasm and confidence in luck. They like to take risks and seize new opportunities.
Sagittarians tend to choose numbers that have to do with travel and personal growth, such as 3s or combinations that reflect their adventurous spirit.

Capricorn (Dec. 22 - Jan. 19): Ambitious strategist
Capricorn, the zodiac sign of Saturn, represents ambition, discipline and strategic planning.

Capricorns approach the lottery with a pragmatic and strategic mindset.

They rely on long-term planning and a disciplined approach to increase their chances of success.

Capricorns may be attracted to numbers associated with stability and success, such as 10, or reflect their crucial combinations.

Aquarius (January 20 – February 18): Innovative Visionary

Aquarius is a solid air sign ruled by Uranus and embodies innovation, independence, and intellectual pursuit.

Aquarius approaches the lottery with unconventional strategies and a unique perspective.

They like to try different approaches and explore new possibilities.

Aquarians may be attracted to numbers associated with progress and social progress, such as 11 or combinations that reflect their visionary nature.

Pisces (February 19 – March 20): Intuitive Dreamer

Pisces is a water sign ruled by Neptune and symbolizes compassion, fantasy, and spiritual connection.

Pisces approaches the lottery with its deep insight and connection with the subconscious mind.

They rely on their dreams and intuitive intuition to make their decisions.

Pisces tend to choose numbers that have to do with spirituality and inner intelligence, such as 12 or a combination that reflects their dreamy and compassionate nature.

Practical guide:

Analyze the unique characteristics of each zodiac sign to gain valuable insights into their potential impact on lottery results.

From the passionate determination of Aries to the intuitive

wisdom of Pisces, each zodiac sign offers a unique way to play the lottery.

Knowing these zodiac signs will help you align your strategy and approach to number picking with the energies associated with each zodiac sign.

III. Discover personalized strategies based on the individual characteristics of the zodiac.

Aries (March 21 - April 19):
As an Aryan, you have a bold and competitive nature.
Show your adventurous spirit and courage when you venture into the lottery.
Trust your instincts, trust your intuitive decisions.
Your lucky numbers can include combinations that reflect your pioneer energy, such as 1, 9, or any number associated with your lucky color, such as bright red or fiery orange.

Taurus (April 20 – May 20):
As a Taurus, you have a pragmatic and patient outlook on life.
Apply this mindset to your lottery predictions by focusing on stability and long-term strategies. Trust your instincts when choosing numbers that relate to material wealth and abundance, such as 4 or a combination that reflects your love of luxury.
Consider incorporating your lucky gemstones, such as emeralds or jade, into your number selection process.

Gemini (May 21 to June 20):
Like Gemini, you have a sharp analytical mind. Use your intelligence and curiosity to explore lottery patterns and strategies. Accept your adaptability and try different approaches.
Consider choosing numbers that have to do with communication and intelligence, such as 5, or combinations that reflect your binary personality.
Pay attention to important dates or lucky numbers associated with lucky days of the week, such as Wednesday.

Cancer (June 21 - July 22):
As a cancer researcher, you are closely connected to your intuition and emotions.
Trust your feelings when it comes to lottery predictions.
Your deep empathy and sensitivity can guide you to the right numbers.
Choose combinations that align with diet and family, such as 2, or numbers that have sentimental value to you.
Consider incorporating lunar cycles and important data related to the moon into your strategy.

Leo (July 23 - August 22):
Like the lion, you exude confidence and creativity. As you approach the lottery, you take on your true nature.
Trust your luck and shine in situations where self-expression is required.
Choose numbers related to success and self-realization, such as 9, or a combination that reflects your courageous and charismatic personality.
Consider adding numbers that relate to your lucky day or a milestone in your life.

Virgo (August 23 - September 22):
As a Virgo, you have a meticulous and analytical mindset.
Pay attention to the details and accuracy of lottery predictions.
Accept its usefulness and rely on statistical analysis, historical data, and pattern recognition.
Focus on purchase order and organization numbers, such as 6, or combinations that reflect your meticulous nature.
Include your lucky color, such as navy blue or earth brown, in the number selection.

Libra (September 23 to October 22):
As Libra, you embody balance, harmony, and diplomacy.
It embraces its collaborative nature when it comes to lottery.
Consider participating in group games or partnerships to increase

your chances of success.

Choose numbers that have to do with beauty and love, such as 7, or combinations that reflect your appreciation for symmetry and aesthetics.

Pay attention to the numbers associated with your lucky numbers or important dates associated with your lucky days.

Scorpio (October 23 - November 21):
Like Scorpio, you possess a deep intensity and intuition.

As you approach the lottery, you embrace your transformative nature.

Trust your instincts and immerse yourself in esoteric practice to improve your predictions.

Consider choosing numbers that are associated with mystery and power, such as 8, or combinations with deep personal meaning.

Pay attention to the numbers that relate to your lucky numbers or milestones in your life.

Sagittarius (November 22 - December 21):
Like Sagittarius, you embody adventure and optimism.

Let your adventurous spirit embrace when you enter the raffle.

Trust in your luck and take advantage of new opportunities.

Choose travel and personal growth numbers, such as 3, or combinations that reflect your passions.

Consider including numbers that relate to your lucky day or numbers that have symbolic value to your sense of adventure.

Capricorn (December 22 – January 19):
As Capricorn, you have ambition and strategic thinking.

Use your convenience and discipline in lottery predictions.

Focus on long-term planning and disciplined approach.

Trust your instincts and choose numbers that are associated with stability and success, such as 10 or a combination that reflects your specific nature. Add numbers that relate to your lucky numbers or milestones in your life.

Aquarius (January 20 to February 18):

As Aquarius, you embody innovation and independence.
Use your unconventional strategy when participating in the lottery.
Think outside the box and explore new possibilities.
Choose numbers that relate to progress and social progress, such as 11, or a combination that reflects your visionary nature.
Pay attention to the numbers that relate to your lucky numbers or the numbers that are important to your spirit of innovation.

Pisces (February 19 – March 20):
As Pisces, you have insight and a deep connection to the subconscious mind.
Believe in your dreams and embrace your compassionate nature as the lottery approaches.
Choose numbers that have to do with spirituality and inner intelligence, such as 12, or combinations with personal meaning.
Consider incorporating the lunar cycle and its associated numbers into your lucky numbers or important dates in your life.

Practical guide:

By discovering custom strategies based on your horoscope profile, you can align lottery predictions with your unique strengths and characteristics.
Whether you're an adventurous Aryan or a meticulous Virgo, adopting your zodiac sign can increase your chances of success.

CHAPTER 7 MOON AND MOON PHASES

Study the phases of the moon and how they are related to lottery luck.

The ever-changing phases of the moon possess a mysterious power that can significantly influence our lottery predictions.

New Moon: Set an intention and visualize success

The new moon marks the beginning of the lunar cycle, when the moon is invisible in the night sky.
It symbolizes a new beginning, a new beginning, and the power of intention.
Harnessing the energy of the new moon can be a powerful tool for lottery predictions.
Here's how you can use the New Moon to increase your lottery luck:

1.   Set intentions: During the new moon phase, take the time to set clear intentions for your lottery adventure. Write down the specific desires, goals, and successes you want to show. Be as detailed as possible and focus on your intention to win the lottery. Imagine claiming the jackpot yourself and experiencing the joy of winning.

2.   Visualization Success: Do a visualization exercise in the new moon phase. Close your eyes and imagine that you are holding your winning ticket in your hand and feel

the excitement and richness of winning the lottery. See the number and moments of celebrations in your favor and see for yourself the possibility of winning the lottery.

Full Moon: Amplify Your Intuition and Trust Your Inner Guidance

The full moon is a powerful and bright phase when the moon is fully illuminated in the night sky.
It represents orgasm, high energy and enlightenment of the subconscious.
The Full Moon is an important time to explore your intuition and trust your inner guidance.
Here's how to use the power of the full moon in the lottery for your luck:

1.	Heightened Insight: During the full moon phase, your intuition is amplified. Look for intuitive ideas, dreams, or clues that might guide you in your lottery predictions. Trust your intuition and let your intuition guide you.

2.	Reflection and liberation: The full moon is also a time to reflect and let go of doubts or limiting beliefs that can hinder the success of the lottery. Take a moment to examine any negative thought patterns or fears that might be slowing down your enrichment. Release them to invite positive energy and happy opportunities to the lottery.

New Moon: Build momentum and act

The new moon phases are after the new moon and before the full moon.
It stands for the growth, expansion and dynamism of construction.
This step is ideal for performing actions inspired by lottery predictions.
Here's how you can use the New Moon to increase your lottery luck:

1.	Research and Strategy: During the New Moon

phase, spend time researching lottery strategies, researching past winning numbers, and analyzing statistics. Use this step to develop your unique approach and streamline the number selection process.

2.   Positive affirmations and mindsets: Adopt positive mindsets and affirmations in the new phase. Repeat statements that align with your lottery goals, such as "I'm a lucky lottery winner" or "I'm attracting big prizes and jackpots." Look at the expected results with confidence and motivation.

Fourth: The Moon Disappears: Let Go of Negative Emotions and Let Them Flow

The fading phases of the moon occur after the full moon and before the new moon. It represents an era of liberation, surrender and detachment. Taking advantage of the weakening of the moon phase, you can let go of negative energy or attachment to a specific outcome in the lottery prediction. Here's how you can work with Falling Moon to increase your lottery luck:

1.   Payout results: During times when the moon phase is weakening, practice rejecting certain lottery results. Free all attachment to victory or defeat and surrender to the natural flow of the universe. Trust that the right numbers and opportunities will coincide with sacred moments.

2.   Clean and clean: Use faded phases of the moon to remove energy blockages or negative effects that could harm your happiness. Engage in practices such as applying sage, meditation, or energizing cleansing rituals to purify your energy and make room for positive vibes.

Time between the phases of the moon with a drawing:

In addition to dealing with the energy of the phases of the moon, it is also necessary to match the expected time of the lottery with the time of the actual draw. Here are some guidelines to keep in mind:

1.   New Moon: Take part in a raffle that takes place a few days after the new moon phase. The new moon reset energy can increase your chances of setting new intentions and succeeding in the lottery.

2.   Full Moon: Take part in a raffle that takes place a few days before and after the full moon phase. The high energy of the full moon amplifies your instincts and increases the likelihood of getting lucky in the lottery.

3.   New Moon: Use the ascending phase to research, strategize, and prepare your digital options. Take part in a raffle that takes place during the new moon phase to align your actions with the building moments of this lunar cycle.

4.   Fading Moon: Use the fading phases of the moon to reflect, let go, and disconnect. Take part in a raffle that takes place when the phases of the moon weaken and be guided by the natural energy flows.

Practical guide:

The phases and cycles of the moon have a profound impact on the fate of the lottery.
Understand what each step means.
•   Define the intention and visualize the success,
•   The Full Moon amplifies intuition and is based on inner guidance,
•   The crescent moon creates momentum and works.
•   The fading moon releases negativity and allows flow by balancing lottery predictions with cosmic energy.

Use the power of the crescent moon, full moon and eclipse to influence lottery results.

Full moon and eclipse affect lottery results; The power of the new moon:

The crescent moon represents a powerful time of new beginnings, new beginnings and clear intentions. When it comes to lotteries, the crescent moon has great potential to fulfill your desires. Here's how you can use the power of the crescent moon to influence lottery results:

1.   Set strong intentions: In the new month, take the opportunity to set clear and specific intentions for your lottery business. Write down your goals, aspirations, and the specific successes you want to show. Imagine holding the winning ticket in your hand and experiencing the joy of the lottery. The concentrated energy of the New Moon amplifies your intentions and aligns them with the cosmic forces at work.

2.   Adopt the mindset of abundance: use the energy of the crescent moon to cultivate a mentality of abundance. Let go of any doubts, fears, or limiting beliefs about winning the lottery. Instead, reaffirm your belief in your ability to attract abundance and rely on the support of the universe. Participate in positive affirmation and visualization exercises to strengthen your enrichment mindset.

Full Moon Effects:

The Full Moon is a powerful, transformative phase that brings more energy and enlightenment.
They have a profound impact on our emotions and intuitions; This makes them significant in the field of lottery forecasting.

Here's how you can use full moon effects to improve your lottery results:

1.   Reinforce intuition: The Full Moon

enhances our intuitive abilities and brings hidden ideas to the surface. Pay close attention to your dreams, feelings, and synchronicities around the full moon. Trust your instincts when picking numbers or making lottery-related decisions. Advanced visual guidance guides you to the right decisions and increases your chances of success.

2.　　　　　Liberation and liberation: The full moon also symbolizes liberation and disconnection from what one no longer needs. Use this stage to let go of negative energy, doubt, or attachment to a particular lottery outcome. Surrender to the natural flow of the universe and trust that the right opportunity will be reconciled with sacred time.

The mysterious power of solar eclipses:

Solar and lunar eclipses have an intriguing transformative energy that can significantly affect lottery results.
These celestial events symbolize a mighty change and bring great changes.
Here's how you can harness the mysterious power of solar eclipses to influence your lottery predictions:

1.　　　　Solar eclipse: Solar eclipses represent new beginnings and opportunities for transformation. Now is the perfect time to change your lottery strategy or approach. Use the eclipse energy to reset your intentions and align them with the desired outcome of the lottery. Do visualization exercises that focus on the success of your goals.

2.　　　　　　Lunar eclipse: A lunar eclipse indicates a climax and the triggering of mood patterns or obstacles. They provide opportunities for deep personal and spiritual growth. Use the energy of the lunar eclipse to reflect on emotional attachments or limiting beliefs that could hinder your success. Let them go and invite positive energy and abundance into your life.

Practical guide:

The power of the crescent moon, the full moon and the eclipse to influence the outcome of the lottery cannot be underestimated.
When you understand the unique energies and possibilities that present themselves in these celestial events, you can align your intentions, insights, and strategies with the cosmic forces at work.

Set strong intentions at New Moon, adopt an abundance mindset, and imagine your lottery success.
Amplify your intuition and rely on your inner guidance during the full moon and let go of negative energy or attachments.
Harness the transformative energy of solar eclipses to initiate change and resolve emotional barriers that can hinder lottery success.

Moon phases and cycles: Use the energy of the moon to increase your chances of winning

Understanding the phases of the moon:
The Moon goes through several stages, each of which has its own unique energy and potential impact on the outcome of the lottery. By understanding and adjusting these stages, you can harness the energy of the moon and increase your chances of winning.

1.   New Moon: The new moon marks the beginning of the lunar cycle when the moon is invisible in the night sky. This step represents a new beginning and a new opportunity. This is the perfect time to define your intentions and visualize the success of your lottery. At New Moon, focus on the desired outcome, imagine a win, and set clear intentions for the numbers you want to play.
2.   New Moon: The new moon is the time between the

new moon and the full moon. It stands for growth, expansion and dynamism. As the moon's brightness increases, so does the potential to showcase your lottery desires. Use the growth phase to gather information, study patterns, and refine your digital sorting strategy. Take challenging steps to achieve your goals and stay positive as you prepare for the next lottery draw.

3.	Full Moon: The Full Moon is a time of heightened energy and enlightenment. It symbolizes the pinnacle of performance, clarity and lace. Full moon energy is powerful and can improve your intuitive abilities and decision-making skills. Use this step to trust your instincts, follow your instincts, and make informed decisions when choosing lottery numbers. Full moon energy can align with your intentions and increase your chances of winning.

4.	Waning Moon: The waning moon is the period between the full moon and the new moon. It stands for liberation, letting go and tidying up what is no longer served. At this point, it is important to let go of any doubts, fears, or negative beliefs that could hinder your success in the lottery. Let go of attachment to a certain outcome and succumb to the natural flow of the universe. Release your energy, practice gratitude, and stay positive as you prepare for the next lunar cycle.

Use the moon sign:

In addition to the phases of the moon, the moon constellation also plays a role in making the energy of the moon usable for lottery success. Each moon sign represents different qualities and influences that can affect your happiness. Here are some general characteristics associated with each moon sign:

1.	Moon in Aries: energetic, safe and competitive. Use the Aries Moon to inspire your determination and take calculated risks while playing the lottery.

2.	Toro Luna: down-to-earth, patient and focused. Use the

energy of the Taurus Moon to maintain consistency, maintain your strategy, and patiently wait for the desired outcome.

3.   Moon in Gemini: curious, adaptable and analytical. Moon in Gemini encourages you to explore different options, pick numbers, gather information, and analyze lottery prediction patterns.

4.   The Cancer Moon: intuitive, nourishing, emotionally sensitive. Trust your instincts and listen to your instincts when choosing lottery numbers under the influence of the Cancer Moon.

5.   Leo-Moon: self-confident, creative, enthusiastic. Embrace the energy of the Leo Moon and bring passion and optimism to your lottery endeavors. Trust your luck and let your inner light shine.

6.   Moon in Virgo: attention to detail, practicality and analysis Virgo Moon requires attention to detail, analysis of data, and the application of systematic methods in number selection.

7.   Libra Moon: balance, diplomacy and cooperation. Use the energy of the Libra Moon to seek harmony and balance in your lottery strategy. Consider participating in group games or partnering to increase your chances of winning.

8.   Moon in Scorpio: intense, intuitive and transformative. Harness the transformative energy of the Scorpio Moon and immerse yourself in esoteric practice, trust your instincts and discover hidden ideas that can guide your lottery predictions.

9.   Moon in Sagittarius: adventurous, optimistic and open-minded. Embrace the energy of the Moon in Sagittarius, take bold risks, explore new strategies, and stay positive on your lottery journey.

10.   Moon in Capricorn: ambitious, self-disciplined and pragmatic. The Capricorn Moon encourages you to approach the lottery with strategic thinking, set long-term goals, and focus on your path to success.

11.   Aquarius Moon: Innovation, Independence, Knowledge Use Aquarius' lunar energy to think outside the box, try out unconventional strategies, and incorporate technological advances into your lottery predictions.

12.   Moon in Pisces: intuitive, dreamy and compassionate. Enjoy the intuitive wisdom of Pisces Moon, trust your dreams and inner guidance, and infuse your lottery journey with compassion and positivity.

Practical guide:

Harnessing the energy of the moon significantly increases your chances of winning the lottery.

By knowing the different phases of the moon and organizing its energies, you can set intentions, perform inspiring actions, and let go of limiting beliefs or negative energy.

In addition, incorporating the influence of the moon sign can provide additional information and guidance for your lottery journey.

CHAPTER 8: THE RISING STAR; EXAMINE THE MEANING OF ASCENDING AND ASCENDING SYMBOLS IN LOTTERY PREDICTIONS.

Understand the ascending and ascending order:

The ascending sign, also known as the ascending sign, is the sign of the zodiac that rises on the eastern horizon at the exact moment of its birth.

It represents the mask you're wearing and the image you're projecting onto the world.

In the context of lottery predictions, the ascending sign plays an important role in influencing your approach, behavior, and potential success. Let's examine ascending symbols and their properties:

Ascension Aries:

If you have an aspiring Aries, you have a competitive and fearless nature.
They approach the lottery with a thirst for adventure, looking forward to adventure and bold decisions.
Your confidence and determination can lead you to a favorable outcome.
Consider choosing leadership and vitality numbers that match Aries' growing energy.

The bull is on the rise:

With the rise of Taurus, you have a practical and patient approach to the lottery.
They rely on your perseverance and constant determination to express your desires.
Taurus-ascending individuals are attracted to numbers associated with abundance and material stability.
Consider choosing numbers that match your love of luxury and financial security.

Ascending twins:

Gemini Risers approaches the lottery with an analytical and adaptable mindset.
You enjoy exploring models, researching strategies and trying out different approaches.
Gemini, ascending individuals, are attracted to numbers related to communication and intelligence.
Engage in digital selection techniques that allow for flexibility and exploration.

Cancer is on the rise:

If you have cancer, approach the lottery with sensitivity and intuition.
Your deep connection to emotions and intuition guides your

decisions.

People with rising cancer rates are attracted to the diet and the number of families.

Consider choosing numbers that have sentimental value or reflect your emotional connection to the lottery.

Leo on the rise:

With the rise of Leo, you exude confidence and charisma.
Its real-world presence shines in the field of lottery predictions.
Leo ascendants believe in their happiness and breathe magnetism.
They are attracted to the numbers associated with success and self-realization.
Show your courage and charm in choosing numbers.

Virgo ascending:

Virgo approaches the lottery with meticulousness and attention to detail. His analytical thinking and attention to detail guide his strategy.
Aspiring Virginians are attracted by the numbers associated with order and organization.
Use statistical analysis, historical data, and pattern recognition to improve the number selection process.

Libra has the wind in its sails:

When your Libra rises, you approach the lottery with a desire for balance and harmony. Thrive in situations involving unions or group play.
Libra-growing people are attracted to numbers associated with beauty and love. Consider choosing numbers that reflect your appreciation for symmetry and aesthetics.

Scorpio rises:

Scorpios approach the lottery with intensity and intuition.

You are not afraid to immerse yourself in esoteric practice and trust your instincts.

The ancestors of Scorpio are attracted to numbers associated with mystery and power. Take exercises to improve your intuitive skills and guide the number selection process.

Sagittarius is on the rise:

With the rise of Sagittarius, you embody a spirit of adventure and optimism.

Trust in your luck and seize new opportunities.

Aspiring people in Sagittarius are attracted by the numbers associated with travel and personal growth.

Consider choosing numbers that match your desire to explore and expand.

Capricorn Ascension:

Capricorn elevators approach the lottery with ambition and strategic thinking.

They rely on long-term planning and a disciplined approach to increase your chances of success.

Capricorn ascendants are attracted to the numbers associated with stability and success. Consider choosing numbers that reflect your determination and desire to succeed.

Aquarius Ascendant:

If your Aquarius is on the rise, you will approach the lottery with an innovative and independent mindset.

You like to try out unconventional strategies and explore new possibilities. Individuals ascending to Aquarius are attracted to the numbers associated with progress and social progress.

Take their unique perspective and incorporate technological advances into your number selection process.

Rising fish:

When Pisces ascend, they possess a dreamy and compassionate nature.
Your deep insight and connection with your subconscious mind will determine your lottery predictions.
The ascending individual of Pisces is attracted to numbers related to spirituality and inner intelligence.
When choosing numbers, trust your dreams and intuitive ideas.

Practical guide:

The ascending or ascending horoscope has a significant impact on your approach to the lottery and your chances of success.
Understand the properties of your ascending sign and align your numerical selection strategies and methods with the energies associated with it.
Each ascending zodiac sign has its own unique strengths and qualities that allow you to use them in search of luck in the lottery.
Remember that astrology is a powerful tool, but it goes hand-in-hand with your intentions, actions, and mood.

Rising Star: revealing hidden potentials and talents associated with certain ascending signs

Aries on the Rise: Warrior Spirit

The ancestors of Aries possess a warrior spirit. They have an innate ability to be bold and passionate about responsibility and leadership.
Its natural confidence and initiative make it a fierce competitor in the lottery space.
Use your pioneering strength and courage to master challenges and take calculated risks.
Your potential for success lies in your ability to trust your

instincts, make quick decisions, and maintain unwavering confidence in your lottery efforts.

Ascending Taurus: a solid foundation

With the rise of Taurus, you will have a solid and stable foundation that will bring stability to your lottery activities.
His pragmatism, patience and determination are his greatest asset.
Use your unwavering concentration and perseverance to express your lottery desires.
Your ability to analyze and assess risk can help you make informed decisions about digital options and strategies.
Be confident that you are capable of attracting wealth and financial security, and let your solid foundation lead you to victory.

Gemini on the rise: masters of communication

Gemini, ascending individuals, are endowed with a gift for communication and adaptability.
Your ability to gather information, analyze patterns, and communicate effectively can greatly improve your lottery predictions. Unleash your natural curiosity and versatility to explore different digital options, technologies, and strategies.
His communication skills allow him to share ideas, collaborate with others, and gain valuable information.
Use your charisma, wit, and intellectual abilities to navigate the world of lottery predictions and increase your chances of success.

Cancer Is On the Rise: Intuitive Dietitians

As Cancer increases, you possess deep insight and emotional sensitivity.
Your ability to connect with your emotions and unseen realms can guide you in your lottery predictions.
Adopt your pedagogical nature and trust your instincts.

Its intuitive information can provide valuable advice when choosing numbers or making decisions.

Pay attention to the subtle signs and feelings that appear within you, as they could be the key to achieving profitable results.

Let your compassionate heart and nurturing spirit illuminate your path to lottery success.

Leo on the rise:

A radiant artist

Those who are descended from Leo radiate splendor and charm.

His natural confidence and talent for self-expression make him a magnet in the lottery space.

Embrace your inner interpreter and trust your luck.

Your energy and creative spark can attract opportunities and positive outcomes. Use your charm, charisma and passion to attract the attention of luck and show the desired outcome in the lottery.

Let your light shine and illuminate the path to success.

Virgo ascending:

Meticulous analyzer

With the ascension of Virgo, you possess a meticulous and analytical mindset.

His attention to detail, methodical approach and critical thinking are his greatest strengths in the field of lottery forecasting. Embrace the analytical nature and rely on statistical analysis, historical data, and pattern recognition to streamline the number selection process.

Your ability to spot fine details and recognize patterns can give you an edge in identifying successful combinations.

Trust your meticulous analysis and let its accuracy guide you to make accurate predictions.

Libra has the wind in its sails:

Harmonious diplomats
Libra ascendants have an innate aptitude for harmony, balance, and diplomacy.
Your ability to seek justice, understanding, and cooperation can greatly influence your lottery predictions.
Accept their diplomatic nature and engage in partnerships or group games to increase your chances of success.
His keen sense of aesthetics and sense of beauty can guide him in choosing numbers that resonate with harmony and balance.
Use your charisma, negotiating skills, and ability to see multiple perspectives to navigate the world of lottery with grace and skill.

Scorpio rises:

High-performance transformers
Those who rise in the sign of Scorpio possess a strong and transforming energy.
His deep insight, perseverance, and ability to delve into hidden realms make him a powerful force in the field of lottery prediction. Adopt your intuitive style and trust your intuition when choosing numbers.
Your ability to discover hidden ideas and explore esoteric practices can lead you to victory.
Allow yourself to embark on the transformative lottery journey and trust that your strong energy will lead you to the desired outcome.

Sagittarius is on the rise:

Optimistic adventurer
With the rise of Sagittarius, you embody a spirit of adventure and optimism.
His belief in happiness, abundance, and new possibilities drives his lottery predictions. Unleash your natural curiosity and desire to discover unique digital decision-making strategies.
Their optimism and enthusiasm attract positive energy and

opportunities.

Embrace the adventures of the lottery journey by taking bold risks and maintaining a positive attitude.

Trust your immeasurable nature and let your adventurous spirit lead you to victory.

Capricorn Ascension:

Ambitious strategist

Capricorn elevators have ambitious and strategic thinking.

His disciplined approach, long-term planning, and determination make him a strong player in the lottery space.

Take advantage of practicality and focus on strategic digital sorting techniques.

Your ability to set clear goals and achieve them will increase your chances of success.

Believe in your ability to demonstrate stability and success through disciplined action, and let your strategic thinking lead you to victory.

Aquarius Ascendant:

Innovative visionaries

With the rise of Aquarius, you embody the spirit of innovation and vision.

Their unique perspective, unconventional strategies, and technical knowledge can revolutionize your lottery predictions.

Embrace your personality and think outside the box when choosing numbers.

Engage in experimental methodologies and integrate technological advances into your strategy.

Your vision beyond tradition can lead to unexpected discoveries and triumphs. Embrace your innovative nature and let your vision guide you to lottery success.

Pisces on the rise: intuitive dreamer

Pisces ascendants possess a dreamy and intuitive nature.

Your deep connection to the subconscious mind and your spiritual perception can greatly influence your lottery predictions.

Adopt your intuitive style and make your dreams come true when choosing numbers.

Let your imagination and compassion lead you to numbers that have personal meaning or reflect your spiritual beliefs.

Your ability to tap into the collective unconscious can uncover hidden messages and lead you to victorious outcomes.

Practical guide:

Uncovering hidden potentials and talents associated with certain ascending signs allows you to explore your unique strengths and abilities in the field of lottery prediction.

By understanding and embracing the qualities that your ascending sign gives you, you can refine your strategies, leverage your innate talents, and increase your chances of success.

Use strategies based on ascending constellations and compatible with favorable cosmic energies.

Rising Aries: Seize the moment

If you have an aspiring Aries, you have a bold and competitive spirit.

To align yourself with favorable cosmic energies, embrace your natural inclination to act and seize the moment.

Your ascending horoscope strategy involves taking decisive and calculated risks.

Trust your instincts when choosing numbers and trust your decisions.

Embrace the dynamic energy of a blooming Aries and approach the lottery with a fearless attitude. Your ability to act quickly and decisively can align you with the cosmic energy that underlies your success.

Rising Taurus: patience and perseverance

When the bull rises, you have a patient and determined nature.
In order to align yourself with favorable cosmic energies, adopt their inherent qualities of patience and perseverance.
Your upstream horoscope strategy involves a long-term approach to the lottery.
Rely on consistency and the power of continuous improvement.
Take the time to study patterns, analyze historical data, and refine the process of number picking.
By staying true to your ascending Taurus nature, you can align yourself with the cosmic energy that rewards patience and perseverance.

Gemini Rising: Adaptability and Versatility

Gemini ascending individuals are adaptable and versatile.
To align yourself with favorable cosmic energies, embrace your natural curiosity and flexibility. Their strategy of ascending symbols involves exploring different number selection techniques and adapting to new approaches.
Participate in the research, explore different methods and try different strategies. Harness the power of communication by asking others for advice and ideas.
By staying adaptable and open-minded, you can align yourself with the cosmic energies that support versatility and adaptability.

Cancer is on the rise: trust your instincts

When you have cancer, you have a deep intuition and emotional sensitivity.
To align yourself with the favorable cosmic energy, accept your intuition and trust your intuition.
Your bottom-up strategy is to listen to your feelings when choosing numbers.

Pay attention to your dreams, synchronicity, and subtle clues to the universe.

Create a sacred space where you can connect with your intuition and receive guidance.

By respecting your ascending intuition of Cancer, you can align yourself with the cosmic energy that underlies your intuitive intuition.

Leo Rising: Self-confidence and self-development

With the rise of Leo, you exude confidence and charisma.
To align yourself with favorable cosmic energies, embrace your inner light and self-expression.
Your ascending horoscope strategy involves developing a positive attitude and exuding self-confidence.
Trust your luck and be passionate about your lottery business.
Use creative visualization techniques to express your desires.
Say thank you for your past victories and celebrate your current successes.
By combining the energies of the Leo ascendant, you can align yourself with the cosmic energies that support self-confidence and self-expression.

Ascent of the Jungfrau: analytical accuracy

Aspiring Virginians possess an analytical and precise mindset.
According to the favorable cosmic energies, accept their attention to detail and methods of analysis.
Their bottom-up strategy involves meticulous analysis of numerical patterns, statistics, and historical trends.
Pay attention to the smallest details and use a systematic approach to refine the process of number selection.
Rely on the power of methodical analysis and accuracy.
By staying true to your ascending Virgo nature, you can align yourself with cosmic energies that reward analytical accuracy.

Libra Rising: Collaboration and Harmony

As your Libra increases, you have a natural tendency towards cooperation and harmony.
In order to stay in tune with the favorable cosmic energies, adopt their diplomatic nature and seek partnerships.
Their ascending horoscope strategy involves participating in group matches or forming alliances with others. Collaborate with like-minded people and increase your chances of success.
Look for balance and harmony in the selection of numbers, consider the views of others and find common ground.
By embracing the spirit of cooperation and harmony, you can align yourself with the cosmic energies that support the common efforts.

Ascending Scorpio: intensity and transformation

With the appearance of Scorpio, you possess a strong and transformative energy.
To align yourself with favorable cosmic energies, embrace your deep insight and embrace transformation.
Your ascending horoscope strategy is to immerse yourself in esoteric practices and use your intuitive insights.
When choosing numbers, trust your instincts and remain open to your inner transformation. Embrace the power to let go and let go of any limiting beliefs or fears that might be holding you back.
By embracing your increasing intensity in Scorpio, you can align yourself with the cosmic energies that support the profound transformations.

Sagittarius on the rise: optimism and adventure

Sagittarius' aspiring individual personifies an adventurous spirit and optimism.
In order to stay in tune with the favorable cosmic energy, accept your belief in happiness and abundance. Your ascending horoscope strategy is to maintain a positive attitude and embark on new adventures. Embrace the element of surprise in number selection.

Explore different strategies and venture boldly. Play with a thirst for adventure and trust in the rich possibilities that the universe offers.

By staying true to your ascending Sagittarius nature, you can align yourself with the cosmic energies that support optimism and adventure.

Capricorn Rise: Strategy and Discipline

If you have a Capricorn on the rise, you have a strategic and disciplined mindset.

To align with favorable cosmic energies, accept their expediency and long-term planning.

Your strategy for an ascending horoscope is to set clear goals and be rigorous when choosing your numbers.

Create a structured routine to examine patterns, analyze data, and refine your strategy.

He believes in the power of consistency and disciplined action. By embracing your ascending strategy and discipline in Capricorn, you can align yourself with the cosmic energy that rewards direct effort.

Aquarius Rising: innovation and uniqueness

The emergence of the individual Aquarius personifies innovation and uniqueness.

In order to keep up with the favorable cosmic energies, unconventional approaches should be pursued and technological advances should be adopted.

Their ascending horoscope strategy involves incorporating innovative technologies and thinking outside the box into the number selection process.

Discover new strategies, try out-of-the-box methods, and use technology to improve your predictions.

Embrace your personality and harness the power of visionary thinking.

By staying true to your ascending Aquarius nature, you can align yourself with the cosmic energies that support innovation and uniqueness.

Fish Rising: Imagination and Intuition

When Pisces increase, they possess a dreamy and intuitive nature. To stay in tune with the favorable cosmic energy, let yourself be inspired by your imagination and intuition.
Your ascending horoscope strategy is to explore your creative imagination and rely on your intuitive ideas.
Use visualization techniques to express your desires and listen to their intuitive whispers when choosing numbers.
Use the power of the symbols and hidden messages they can have.
By embracing Pisces' growing imagination and intuition, you can align yourself with the cosmic energies that support your vision.

Practical guide
Use bottom-up sign strategies that align with favorable cosmic energies that are specific to your unique qualities and strengths.
By understanding the inherent qualities of the ascending sign combined with strategies tailored to the ascending sign, you can improve your lottery prediction and increase your chances of success.
Combine your astrological knowledge, insights, personalization strategies, and other techniques explored in this book to optimize your ability to accurately predict lottery outcomes.
In the next chapter we dive into the fascinating world of planetary transits.

CHAPTER 9: ASTROLOGICAL TIME

Learn more about the importance of astrological weather in lottery prediction.

First, the cosmic dance of the planets:
Astrology recognizes that celestial bodies, including planets, are constantly dancing in the sky.
Each planetary movement and alignment has its own energy and influence.
By learning cosmic dances and aligning your lottery activities with these celestial rhythms, you can tap into the soothing energy that underpins your success.

Decline and transit
A key aspect of astrological chronology is the phenomenon of retrograde transit. Retrograde occurs when a planet appears to move away from Earth's perspective in its orbit.
In retreat, the energy of the earth becomes more introspective and internalized.
A transit, on the other hand, refers to the current position of a planet in relation to its natal chart.

When it comes to lottery predictions, the deterioration and transit of key planets could have significant implications.
Retrograde provides a period of reflection, review, and re-evaluation.
It's time to adjust your strategy, review previous models, and rethink your approach to digital sorting.
Transitions, on the other hand, show your current planetary

positions and how they interact with your birth chart.

By studying these transits, you can gain insights into favorable cosmic energies that align with your lottery activity.

2.		Planetary aspects:

The planetary aspect, which refers to the angle at which planets form relative to each other, also plays an essential role in astrological time.

Each aspect has its own energy and effect.

Some aspects can increase happiness and favorable outcomes, while others can present challenges or obstacles.

By learning about planetary aspects and their impact on the horoscope chart, you can plan lottery events to align with the most beneficial planetary impacts.

For example, the favorable appearance between the Moon and Venus may indicate a time of greater happiness and harmony, making it a good time to play the lottery.

Similarly, incorporating the beneficial aspects of Jupiter, expanding and abundant planets, can increase your chances of success.

By exploring the planetary aspects and choosing the perfect time to participate in the lottery event, you can maximize your chances and improve your lottery prediction.

3.		Lunar and solar eclipses:

Lunar and solar eclipses have great significance in astrology and can have a huge impact on lottery predictions.

Solar eclipses mark a time of strengthening and transformation of energy.

Lunar eclipses occur during the full moon phase, when the Earth's shadow obscures the moon, while solar eclipses occur during the new moon phase, when the moon obscures the sun.

During a solar eclipse, cosmic energy increases and the potential for profound changes and discoveries is amplified.

Solar eclipses are powerful gateways to change and opportunity. By focusing on the eclipse and its alignment with the horoscope chart, you can use this amplified energy to your advantage.

During these powerful times, engage in deep reflection, develop strong intentions, and take thought-provoking actions to align your lottery efforts with the transformative energy of the eclipse.

4.   Personalized schedule:

While general astrological guides provide valuable information, it is important to consider your unique horoscope and the position of each planet.

Your horoscope contains blueprints of your life energy, and certain alignments and planetary aspects can have a greater impact on your predictions and lottery calendar.

To determine a custom time for a lottery event, consult with an experienced astrologer or use advanced astrology software to analyze your horoscope and provide information about the most favorable time for the lottery event.

Consider factors such as transits of key planets, aspects that affect lucky planets such as Jupiter, and the alignment of eclipses with astrological horoscopes.

In addition to astrological time, it is crucial to listen to your intuition and trust your inner guidance.

Your intuition can provide valuable information and push you to act at the right time.

Pay attention to synchronicity, dreams and feelings that can lead you to the opportune moment of lottery prediction.

5.   Time and intention:

Astrological time isn't just about choosing the right time to play the lottery. It's also about aligning your intentions with cosmic energy.

Before participating in a lottery event, take the time to set a clear intention and visualize the desired outcome. By aligning your intentions with cosmic energy, you can create a powerful synergy to support your efforts.

It is important to note that astrological weather does not guarantee winning the lottery.
It improves your understanding of cosmic influences and guides you on when you should participate in lottery events.
Ultimately, their behavior, mentality, and random factors play an important role in determining outcomes.
Astrology is a tool that focuses on the cosmic energies that promote your success.

Practical guide:
Understanding the importance of weather in lottery prediction is a key aspect of making the most of astrology's potential.
By aligning your lottery activities with celestial, retrograde rhythms, transits, planetary aspects, and eclipse energies, you can tap into the favorable cosmic energy that underlies your success.
Remember to consider your horoscope as unique and consult an astrology expert for personalized weather information.

CHAPTER 10: EXPLORE THE PLANETARY CYCLES, PROGRESS, AND TRANSIT INVOLVED IN THE STRATEGIC LOTTERY.

1.   Planetary period:

Planetary cycles play an important role in astrology and provide valuable information about the ebb and flow of cosmic energy.
Each planet has its own specific period, which indicates its journey through the zodiac and its return to its original location.
By following these cycles, periods of high energy can be identified for a particular planet, creating the right time to participate in the lottery.

The cycle of Jupiter, for example, lasts about 12 years, marking an important period of expansion, abundance, and happiness.
After the return of Jupiter, the probability of a favorable lottery outcome increases if Jupiter coincides with its birth position in its birth chart. Think of this time as a happy time and take advantage of the opportunities that come your way.

Similarly, the Saturn cycle spans about 29 years and symbolizes long-term lessons, discipline, and rewards.

Consider the transit and evolution of Saturn in the natal chart to determine the period in which your lottery efforts are likely to bear fruit.

Balancing your participation in the lottery with the supportive energy of Saturn can lead to great prizes and lasting success.

2.   Order:

Advances in astrology refer to the symbolic trajectory of your birth chart over time.

As the planets continue their journey, their primordial stars move forward, revealing new aspects of their potential and influencing different areas of their lives.

The advanced aspect can provide valuable information about the favorable time of participation in the lottery.

By analyzing the progress of key planets such as Jupiter, Venus, and the Moon, you can better understand the periods when the energetic alignment works in your favor. The progressive aspects that affect these planets can indicate better times and positive lottery results.

Think of these periods as the chances of maximizing lottery success.

3.   Transit:

Transits – the current positions of the planets in relation to their natal chart – provide valuable insights into the role of cosmic energy in your life.

By focusing on transits, especially those involving lucky planets like Jupiter and Venus, you can strategically plan your participation in the raffle.

For example, if Jupiter forms a harmonious appearance with its planet or natal horn, it means a period of increased happiness and favorable opportunities.

Combine your lottery activities with these promising crossovers to increase your chances of success. Venus is a beautiful and rich planet, and it can also have positive effects if it forms beneficial aspects with its parent star. Use these moments to your advantage and enter the lottery with confidence.

4.   Take part in the strategic raffle:

In order to participate strategically in the lottery, it is essential to combine knowledge of planetary cycles, progress and transits.

By aligning your lottery activities with the favorable cosmic energies indicated by these astrological factors, you can increase your chances of success.

Start by following the cycles of Jupiter, Saturn, and other major planets in the natal chart. Note the periods when these planets coincide with their natal positions or form favorable aspects that indicate potential opportunities for favorable outcomes.

Take these periods as a window of cosmic support and seize the moment to enter the lottery.

Also note the progress and transit involved in happy planets such as Jupiter and Venus.

These moments offer maximum happiness and ample potential, making it an ideal time to participate in strategic raffles.

Integrate these periods into your lottery strategy and maximize your odds.

Integrate horoscope time into your

5.   Lottery Strategy:

To use astrological time effectively in your lottery strategy, you should consider the following steps:

Study your birth chart: Take a look at your planet, your home, and aspects of childbirth. Identify important planets that affect happiness, abundance, and financial problems, such as Jupiter and

Venus.

Track planetary cycles: Monitor the cycles of important planets such as Jupiter and Saturn. Make a note of the periods when they coincide with the place of birth in the birth chart, as these times have the potential to lead to greater happiness and positive outcomes.

Analytical Advances: Explore the progressive aspects of lucky planets in the natal chart. If these planets form harmonious aspects with their planetary or birth horns, be careful, as these periods indicate the favorable energy of participating in the lottery.

Watch out for auspicious transits: Keep an eye out for current transits of lucky planets like Jupiter and Venus. When these planets form beneficial aspects with their parent stars, it marks a period of greater happiness. Align your lottery activities with these crossovers to increase your chances of success.

Trust your instincts: Even though the astrological weather gives valuable advice, you should always listen to your instincts. Pay attention to synchronicity, dreams and feelings that can lead you to the opportune moment of participating in the lottery. Trust your inner wisdom when making decisions that align with cosmic energy.

Combine time with other strategies: astrological time is only one piece of the puzzle. Combine this with the custom strategies, digital sorting techniques, and other tools explored in this book. By integrating multiple methods, you can create a comprehensive and powerful lottery strategy.

Practical guide:
Astrological weather, including planetary cycles, progression, and transits, is an invaluable tool for participating in the strategic lottery.
By aligning your lottery activities with the cosmic energy

indicated by these astrological factors, you can increase your chances of success.

Don't forget to study your natal chart, track planetary cycles, analyze progress, and observe the auspicious transits of the lucky planets.
Combine this knowledge with your intuition and other lottery strategies to create a comprehensive approach.
Astrology can serve as a guide for you to understand cosmic influences and make informed decisions.
Although lottery winnings are not guaranteed,
Improve your understanding of favorable cosmic energies and direct your time to participate in the lottery.

CHAPTER 11.
DEVELOP CUSTOM TIMING TECHNIQUES TO INCREASE YOUR CHANCES OF WINNING.

1. Know your birth chart:

In order to develop individual timing techniques, it is important to have a deep understanding of your birth charts.

Your birth chart is a model of the cosmic energy that existed when you were born.

It reveals the position of the planets, the aspects in which they were formed, and the houses that inhabit them. By analyzing these elements, you can gain valuable insight into timing techniques that resonate with your unique energy.

II. Identify your lucky planet:

In your natal chart, some planets may be more important in terms of good luck and happiness.

Study the positions and aspects of planets such as Jupiter, Venus, and the Moon in your horoscope.

These planets are often associated with happiness, abundance, and intuitive ideas. When you recognize your lucky planet, you can focus on timing techniques that align with your energy.

Use the indicator of your planet:
Each zodiac sign is ruled by a specific planet, which gives this constellation its unique qualities.
Knowing the planetary scales in the natal chart, you can determine the favorable period for participating in the lottery.
For example, if your ascendant is ruled by Venus, align your time strategy with the energy of Venus, such as when Venus passes through the House of Fortune on your map or forms aspects of harmony with other planets.

3. Say hello to the transit of the happy planet:

Transits of lucky planets such as Jupiter and Venus can greatly influence lottery predictions.
Follow the movements of these planets and observe when they form beneficial aspects with planets or birth horns.
These crosses indicate periods of happiness and potential abundance.
Align your lottery entry with these cheap crossovers to increase your chances of winning.

Follow the rhythm of your moon:

The Moon has a significant impact on our mood and intuition.
By focusing on the lunar cycle and its interaction with the natal chart, it is possible to develop custom synchronization techniques.
Observe the cycles of the new moon and full moon and how they coincide with the planets and lucky houses in the natal chart.
These phases of the moon reinforce your intuitive ideas and help you choose the right moments to participate in the lottery.

5. Trust your instincts:

In astrology, intuition plays an essential role in measuring time. Trust your inner feelings and advice when organizing lottery events.

If a certain day or time suits you, even if it does not coincide with the traditional astrological moments,

It can have its own energetic resonance. Remember that astrology is a tool, but your intuition is a powerful compass that can guide you at the best time for the lottery.

6. Create a personal ceremony:

Personal rituals can help you regulate cosmic energy and improve your timing.

Customize your ritual to suit your birth chart and preferences.

This can be lighting candles, meditating on your lucky gemstones, or reciting wishes that correspond to the desired outcome of the lottery. These rituals create a sacred space where you can focus your intentions and energies on the success of the lottery.

VII. Experiment and Adjust: As with any technique, it's important to experiment and perfect your custom timing technique.

Astrology provides structure, but it's up to you to figure out what best suits your unique energies and preferences.

Record the results of the experiment in time and, if necessary, change the method.

Some periods can produce better results than others, and with trial and error, you can improve your timing skills to increase your chances of winning.

Combine time with other strategies:

Custom timing techniques, while powerful, are only one piece of the puzzle. Combine them with other lottery strategies such as digital selection techniques, visualization, and positive affirmations.

By integrating multiple approaches, you can create a comprehensive, synergistic lottery strategy that increases your chances of success.

IX. Endure and enjoy the process:
While timing technology can improve lottery predictions, it's important to maintain a balanced view.
Lottery results involve random factors and unforeseen circumstances.
Don't forget to keep your feet on the ground and approach the lottery with fun and curiosity. Embrace the process and celebrate small victories along the way.
By cultivating a positive attitude, you can attract positive energy and increase the overall success rate of the lottery.

Practical guide:
By developing custom timing techniques, you can increase your chances of winning the jackpot. By learning about your horoscope, identifying your lucky planet, using the planetary ruler, accepting the transit of the lucky planet, following the lunar rhythm, trusting your instincts, creating personal rituals, and trying different approaches, you can adjust your time strategy according to your unique energy.

Combine these techniques with other lottery strategies to create a holistic approach that maximizes your chances of success.
Remember that astrology is a tool that can guide you, but at the end of the day, your behavior, mindset, and random factors all play a role in lottery results.
Use astrology to align yourself with favorable cosmic energies, but also be open to unexpected opportunities and be confident on the journey.

CHAPTER 12.
INTUITION AND PROPHECY:

Use the intuitive power of astrologers to get lottery information.

First, the power of intuition in astrology:
Intuition is an innate talent of every astrologer.

It is a form of direct knowledge that goes beyond logical reasoning and explores the subtle energies of the universe.
When predicting lottery outcomes, your intuition can be a powerful tool.
It allows you to access hidden information, identify underlying patterns, and gain insights beyond what's obvious on the surface.
By relying on your intuitive skills and refining them, you can greatly improve your ability to make accurate predictions in the lottery.

II. Connection with divine guidance:

As an astrologer, it is important to maintain a deep connection with divine guidance.
This connection opens the door to intuitive information.
Engage in practices such as meditation, prayer, or rituals to calm your mind, open your heart, and create a sacred space for divine guidance.
Allow yourself to be a container for higher intelligence so that it can flow into intuitive awareness.

When you enter this state of acceptance, you can effortlessly reach out to news and ideas about lottery results.

Third, the role of divination technology:

Divination techniques can further support your intuitive ideas as an astrologer.
These techniques serve as tools to guide divine guidance and provide an additional layer of information for lottery predictions.
Divination tools such as tarot cards, oracle cards, pendulums, or astrological dice can help you gain deeper insights and clarify certain questions related to the lottery.

By incorporating divination techniques into your practice, you can unlock hidden knowledge and improve your understanding of lottery results.

4. The art of symbolic interpretation:

Symbols are a language of the universe, and as an astrologer, you can interpret these symbols and extract valuable information. Pay attention to the symbols that appear in your dreams, visions, or daily life, as they may contain important information related to lottery predictions.
Develop the practice of symbolic interpretation by studying various symbol systems such as astrology, numerology, and mythology.
Expand your library of symbols and their meanings to uncover hidden information about lottery results.

5. Listen to the subtle whisper:

Intuition often speaks to us through subtle whispers, nudges, or feelings.
As an astrologer, it is crucial to regulate these subtle signals.
Pay attention to physical sensations, emotions, and intuitive premonitions that emerge during astrological analysis.

These intuitive tips can provide valuable clues and guide you to the most accurate predictions.
Build confidence in intuitive impressions and incorporate them into your lottery ideas.

6. Balance between intuition and astrology

Although intuition plays an important role in lottery prediction,
It must be balanced by a thorough astrological analysis.
Use your astrological knowledge and understanding of planetary positions, aspects, and transits as a solid foundation for your intuitive ideas.
Combine your intuitive impressions with the objective data displayed in the horoscope or in the current horoscope settings.

This integration of intuition and astrological analysis creates a holistic approach to lottery prediction where rational and intuitive abilities work together harmoniously.

VII Develop your practice of intuitive astrology:

To improve your intuitive astrological practice of lottery ideas, consider the following steps:

1. Develop self-awareness: Discover your intuitive process. Think about how your intuition behaves towards you and identify patterns or symbols that often appear in your intuitive experience. This self-awareness strengthens your intuitive connection and allows you to make better use of the intuitive cues of lottery predictions.

2. Create a sacred space: Designate a specific space for your intuitive astrology practice. Make it a sanctuary where you can connect with divine guidance. Remove all distractions in the room and inject them deliberately, whether through candles, crystals, or other sacred objects that resonate with you. This sacred space is a gateway to intuitive ideas.

3. Do daily exercises: Take time each day to connect with your intuition and get guidance. This can include meditation, journaling, or any other practice that helps calm the mind and open intuitive channels. The consistency of these practices will deepen your intuitive skills and allow you to get more accurate information about the lottery.

4. Practice active listening: Actively listen to intuitive whispers during astrological analysis. Pay attention to assumptions, feelings, or intuitive symbols that pop up. Trust these subtle messages and let them guide you in your interpretation. Practice discernment and validate your intuitive ideas against astrological data to ensure accuracy.

5. Use divination tools: Incorporate divination tools into your intuitive astrological practice to improve your understanding. Tarot, oracle cards, or pendulums can provide additional guidance to help you confirm or clarify your intuitive impressions. Choose guessing tools that resonate with you and incorporate them into your lottery prediction process.

6. Trust the process: Trust the wisdom and guidance that flows through your intuitive practice of astrology. Confidence in your ability to gain superior knowledge and make accurate predictions. Let go of any doubt or doubt that could hinder your intuitive abilities. Trust that the process will give you more freedom to provide intuitive information and guide you to more accurate lottery predictions.

Practical guide:

Using the intuitive skills of an astrologer is a powerful tool for obtaining lottery information.

By developing your intuition, connecting with divine guidance, incorporating divination techniques, interpreting symbols, and actively listening for subtle whispers, you can unlock a deeper understanding and accuracy in your lottery predictions.

Remember to balance your intuition with in-depth astrological analysis and use your knowledge of planetary positions, aspects, and transitions as a solid foundation.

Intuition is a divine gift that, when combined with astrology, can provide insight into lottery results.

Trust your intuitive abilities, practice regularly, and create a sacred space to receive divine instruction.

As you develop your intuitive practice of astrology, your lottery predictions become more subtle, accurate, and aligned with cosmic energy.

CHAPTER 12. INTEGRATE DIVINATION TOOLS SUCH AS TAROT, NUMEROLOGY, OR PENDULUM MEASUREMENTS TO IMPROVE PREDICTIONS.

1.   Astrological Time: Integrating Divination Tools to Improve Predictions

The power of divination in astrology:

For centuries, divination tools have been used to gain hidden knowledge, gain clarity, and receive guidance from the spiritual realm.

When combined with astrology, divination tools provide a unique perspective and an additional layer of information to support

lottery predictions.
These tools help you explore the collective intelligence of the universe and interpret the symbols and information that emerge in the process.

Tarot lottery at a glance:

Tarot cards are a popular divination tool that can provide good information about lottery results. Each card carries its own symbolism, archetypal energy and message.
With tarot spreads designed specifically for lottery predictions, you can gain a deeper understanding of the energy and potential outcomes at stake.

When you use tarot cards to get lottery information, focus on specific topics related to your lottery efforts.
Shuffle the game and draw cards that represent different aspects of the problem, such as the overall energy of the lottery, potential challenges, favorable opportunities, or number selection suggestions. Explain the meaning of the letters in the context of your question and trust the intuitive message they convey.

Numerological predictions and lottery:

Also, numerology, the study of numbers and their swinging meaning can improve lottery predictions. By analyzing the numerological value of important data, numbers related to your birth chart, or numbers that repeat in your life, you can better understand their potential impact on lottery results.

To make lottery predictions using numerology, check the vibration characteristics of the numbers and how they match your intentions.
Tell your life path, fate or personal years and explore their significance in relation to participating in the lottery.
Pay attention to recurring numerical patterns and their meanings.

For example, if the number 7 stands out, it may indicate a moment of reflection, analysis and selection of strategic numbers.

Pendulum measurements to drive the lottery:

The pendulum can serve as a powerful tool for getting yes or no answers, providing clarity, and getting intuitive advice.
By asking specific questions about lottery results and observing the movement of the pendulum, you can use its intuitive intelligence and get definitive answers.
To use the pendulum to drive the lottery, be stable and give clear answers with "yes" and "no" by asking calibration questions.
Once you have determined the answers, ask specific questions about participating in the lottery, choose the number or the best time.
Observe the movements of the pendulum, whether it swings back and forth, from left to right, or in a circle, and interpret these movements as an answer to the question.

Combine divination with astrological time:
When combining divination tools with the astrological calendar, you should consider the following steps:

1.	Define your intent: Clearly define your intent to use the guessing tool in lottery prediction. Indicate that you intend to receive specific, in-depth advice that matches your best interests and lottery success.

2.	Choose the right instrument: Choose the guessing tool that appeals to you the most. Whether we are talking about tarot, numerology or pendulum measurements, choose the most relevant and convenient tool. Trust your instincts and choose the tool that best supports your lottery predictions.

3.	Prepare your divinatory space: Create a sacred and focused space for your divinatory practice. Eliminate all distractions and ensure a calm and peaceful environment.

Light candles, burn incense sticks, or use any other ritual element to get into a high state of consciousness.

4.   Ask specific questions: Before you start guessing, ask specific questions about your lottery prediction. The questions should be clear and concise, focusing on areas such as numerical selection, timing, or possible outcomes. Write down your questions to organize them and easily relate to yourself in your divination practices.

5.   Follow your divination process: Perform your chosen divination technique according to your specific instructions. Trust the messages and information conveyed by Ratetools. Document your discoveries and any visual impressions that show up along the way. These results will be a valuable reference for your future lottery predictions.

6.   Analyze and consolidate information: After completing a guessing session, analyze the information obtained. Look for patterns, connections, and correlations between information from divination tools and ideas from astrological times. Find a balance between intuitive impressions and objective astrological data.

7.   Adjust your timing and strategy: Use the information you've gained from guesswork to improve your lottery timing and strategy skills. Adjust your approach based on the advice you receive and align it with the cosmic energies indicated by your astrological analysis. Combine divination knowledge with your knowledge of planetary cycles, transits, and progress to optimize your lottery predictions.

8.   Trust your instincts and take stimulating action: Trust your intuition and the next promptings by combining divination tools with astrological synchronization. Feed your intuitive insights into your decisions and take thought-provoking actions based on the messages you receive. Trust that the universe will support your lottery efforts and that

their intuitive advice will guide you to the most favorable outcome.

Practical guide:

1.   Combining divination tools such as tarot, numerology, or pendulum measurements with astrological weather can greatly improve lottery predictions. These tools provide an additional layer of knowledge that allows you to tap into the collective intelligence of the universe and interpret symbols and information as they appear. Trust your instincts by choosing a puzzle tool that appeals to you and incorporate it into your lottery prediction process.

2.   Set clear intentions, ask specific questions, and create a sacred space for your divination practice. Follow the instructions in your chosen guessing tool to document your results and analyze the information you receive. Combine fortune telling knowledge with your astrological weather knowledge to perfect your lottery strategy. Trust your instincts, take inspirational action, and trust the advice you receive.

3.   Remember that astrology and fortune telling are powerful tools, but they do not guarantee the success of the lottery. They provide guidance and support to help you stay in tune with cosmic energy and make informed decisions. Combine these tips with positive thinking, visualization practices, and gratitude to create a holistic approach to the desired outcome of the lottery. In the next chapter, we'll explore the transformative power of intention and how it can shape your lottery destiny. Get ready to harness the power of your focused intention to unlock the endless possibilities that lie ahead.

III. Embrace the mystical and intuitive aspects of astrology to unlock the mysterious potential of the lottery:

Astrology Moments: Embrace the mysterious and intuitive aspects of astrology to unlock the hidden potential of the lottery
Introduce:
During our fascinating journey through the world of astrology and its connection with lottery predictions, we explore various aspects, including astrological signs, houses, planetary patterns, favorable environments, personalized strategies, moon phases, cycles, ascending signs, strategies based on ascending signs, the meaning of time, planetary cycles, progress and transit, the power of intuition and fortune telling, and the integration of guessing tools for Improving forecasts.

1.   Mysterious connection:
Basically, astrology is a mysterious and sacred art. It invites us to recognize the interdependence of the universe and our existence.
By embracing the mysterious aspects of astrology, we can unlock the hidden potential of the lottery.
This mystical connection forces us to go beyond rational thinking and embrace the realm of intuition and consciousness.

2.   Awakening of intuition:
Intuition is the bridge between the conscious and unconscious realms. It allows us to explore hidden areas of knowledge and gain knowledge that goes beyond logical thinking.
By nourishing and awakening our intuition, we can access the hidden potential of the lottery.
Meditation, mindfulness, and other spiritual practices can help calm the mind and open our hearts to intuitive guidance.
By participating in these practices on a regular basis, we create space for intuition to emerge and guide ourselves in making lottery predictions.
It's important to trust our intuition because it's like a compass that can guide us to the right numbers, deadlines, and strategies to succeed in the lottery.

3.   Adopt synchronicity:

Synchronicity is an important coincidence that occurs in our lives.

They are the way the universe communicates with us, giving us insight and guidance on our path.

When it comes to lotteries, synchronicity can serve as a powerful indicator of hidden potential and favorable outcomes.

Pay attention to the synchronicity of what's happening in your life.

These can manifest as digital patterns, random encounters, or random events that seem to coincide with your lottery efforts.

Keep a journal and record these synchronizations, think about what they might mean and how they relate to your lottery predictions.

Accept these magical events as an affirmation of the universe that will lead you on the right path.

4.   Connection to the Higher Realms:

Astrology invites us to recognize the connection between the heavenly and earthly realms.

By cultivating a connection to a higher realm through prayer, meditation, or rituals, we can tap into the wisdom and guidance of forces in the universe that influence our predictions.

Engage with practices that resonate with you and connect with higher realms. Create sacred rituals that honor the energies of heaven and invite its blessings into your lottery work.

Seek advice from spirit guides, guardian angels, or divine beings who align with your beliefs.

Trust these connections to provide you with great information and support for your lottery journey.

5.   Embodying cosmic energy:

As astrologers, we have the ability to manifest and align with the cosmic energies that affect the lottery.

By consciously adapting to these energies, we become conduits for the flow of mysterious potential.

Study the planetary energies associated with happiness, abundance, and financial success in astrology.
Get an overview of these energies and align yourself with their qualities.
For example, if Jupiter has a significant influence on the success of the lottery, it cultivates qualities such as optimism, expansion and generosity.
Imagine integrating these energies and attracting results that are favorable to the lottery.

6.   Accept the time of astrology:

Embrace the mystical and intuitive aspects of astrology to unlock the hidden potential of the lottery
Introduce:
During our fascinating journey through the world of astrology and its connection with lottery predictions, we explore various aspects, including astrological signs, houses, planetary patterns, favorable environments, personalized strategies, moon phases, cycles, ascending signs, strategies based on ascending signs, the meaning of time, planetary cycles, progress and transit, the power of intuition and fortune telling, and the integration of guessing tools for Improving forecasts.
In this chapter, we will now delve into the mysterious and intuitive aspects of astrology and unlock the hidden potential of the lottery through a deep connection with the universe.
Get ready to enjoy the magical and profound aspects of astrology, explore how to explore mysterious areas, and discover the lottery's untapped potential.

7.   Mysterious connection:

Basically, astrology is a mysterious and sacred art. It invites us to recognize the interdependence of the universe and our existence.
By embracing the mysterious aspects of astrology, we can unlock the hidden potential of the lottery.
This mystical connection forces us to go beyond rational thinking and embrace the realm of intuition and consciousness.

8.   Awakening of intuition:

Intuition is the bridge between the conscious and unconscious realms.

It allows us to explore hidden areas of knowledge and gain knowledge that goes beyond logical thinking.

By nourishing and awakening our intuition, we can access the hidden potential of the lottery.

Meditation, mindfulness, and other spiritual practices can help calm the mind and open our hearts to intuitive guidance.

By participating in these practices on a regular basis, we create space for intuition to emerge and guide ourselves in making lottery predictions.

It's important to trust our intuition because it's like a compass that can guide us to the right numbers, deadlines, and strategies to succeed in the lottery.

9.   Adopt synchronicity:

Synchronicity is an important coincidence that occurs in our lives.

They are the way the universe communicates with us, giving us insight and guidance on our path. When it comes to lotteries, synchronicity can serve as a strong indicator of hidden potential and favorable outcomes.

Pay attention to the synchronicity of what's happening in your life.

These can manifest as digital patterns, random encounters, or random events that seem to coincide with your lottery efforts.

Keep a diary and record these synchronizations, think about what they might mean and how they relate to your lottery predictions.

Accept these magical events as an affirmation of the universe that will lead you on the right path.

10.   Connection to the Higher Realms:

Astrology invites us to recognize the connection between the heavenly and earthly realms.

By cultivating a connection to a higher realm through prayer, meditation, or rituals, we can tap into the wisdom and guidance of forces in the universe that influence our predictions.

Engage with practices that resonate with you and connect with higher realms. Create sacred rituals that honor the energies of heaven and invite its blessings into your lottery work.

Seek advice from spirit guides, guardian angels, or divine beings who align with your beliefs.

Trust these connections to provide you with great information and support for your lottery journey.

11.   Embodying cosmic energy:

As astrologers, we have the ability to manifest and align with the cosmic energies that affect the lottery.

By consciously adapting to these energies, we become conduits for the flow of mysterious potential.

Study the planetary energies associated with happiness, abundance, and financial success in astrology.

Get an overview of these energies and align yourself with their qualities. For example, if Jupiter has a significant influence on the success of the lottery, it cultivates qualities such as optimism, expansion and generosity.

Imagine integrating these energies and attracting results that are favorable to the lottery. Hug

CHAPTER 13:
PRACTICAL ADVICE
AND STRATEGIES:

Practical tips for participating in the lottery, based on astrological findings.

I. Practical advice and strategies for applying astrological knowledge to increase participation in the lottery

1.　　Understand your horoscope

Your horoscope is a model of your unique cosmic energy. Knowing your horoscope will help you identify favorable planetary positions and aspects that may indicate the potential success of the lottery. Note the locations of lucky planets such as Jupiter and Venus, as well as aspects related to the Sun and Moon. These investments can provide valuable information about your assets and wealth.

2.　　Choose a good time:

Astrology gives valuable tips on how to organize your time to participate in the lottery. Take into account the favorable aspects and transit that occur during a certain period of time. For example, if Jupiter is good for your birth sun, then this could be a good time to buy a lottery ticket. Again, pay attention to the difficult aspects and avoid getting involved in these times.

3.　　Alignment with lunar energy:

The phases of the moon and the cycle of phases of the moon have a profound impact on our lives, including lottery results. Watch out for new and full moons, as they carry powerful energies that amplify your intentions and achievements. Set clear intentions for lottery success at new moon, while the full moon is ideal for letting go of doubts or fears. Use the lunar cycle to control your participation in the lottery.

4.   Follow its ascending sign:

Your ascending sign is the sign that ascended to the eastern horizon when you were born. It represents your external personality and the impression you make on others. Use your ascending horoscope as a guide to choose numbers that match your characteristics or play a specific lottery game. For example, if your Leo is on the rise, you should choose numbers related to creativity, self-expression, and boldness.

5.   Selecting numbers by numerology:

Numerology, the study of numbers and the meaning of their vibrations can help you choose numbers for participation in the lottery. Calculate your resume number, destination number, or personal year and research their meaning. Consider incorporating these numbers into your number selection strategy, choosing numbers that match yours, or tapping into numbers associated with luck and abundance.

6.   Set a clear intent:

The power of intention cannot be underestimated. Clearly state your intention to succeed in the lottery, introduce yourself as a winner and experience the excitement of getting the desired result. This conscious intention sends a powerful message to the universe and aligns your energy with the frequency of abundance and prosperity.

7.   Practice positive affirmations:

Affirmations are positive affirmations that reinforce your beliefs and intentions. Use statements such as "I am a magnet for lottery prizes", "I attract wealth and financial wealth" or "I am ready to accept lottery blessings". Repeat these affirmations every day with beliefs and beliefs to program your subconscious mind to attract positive lottery results.

8.   Develop a positive mindset:

Maintaining a positive attitude is essential for the success of the lottery. Develop optimism, gratitude and confidence in your ability to achieve the desired results. Let go of any limiting doubts or beliefs that may hinder your progress. Be with positive people, environments, and resources that support your positive attitude.

9.   Practice self-care for health and energy:

Taking care of your physical, mental, and emotional well-being is crucial when participating in the lottery. Practice self-care practices such as exercise, meditation, adequate rest, and healthy eating. Manage your energy by allowing yourself to be positively influenced, avoid negative or stressful environments, and respect your intentions.

10.   Trust your instincts:

Your intuition is a powerful tool when it comes to participating in the lottery. Trust your inner guidance and listen to their feelings when deciding what games to play, when to play, and what numbers to choose. Pay attention to the intuitive drive, synchronicity, and subtle information of the universe. Your intuition can provide valuable information that complements your astrological knowledge.

11.   Keep expectations realistic:

While astrology can provide guidance, it's important to maintain realistic expectations about lottery results. There is no guarantee of winning the lottery, it must be approached with a balanced perspective. Focus on the joy of participating, the excitement of the opportunities, and the personal growth that comes from the participation process. Avoid focusing too much on the outcome, and remember that astrology is just one of the many tools that increase your chances.

12.   Celebrate small victories:
Even if you don't hit the jackpot, celebrate the small winners or wins along the way. Recognize and appreciate the progress you've made, whether it's by winning smaller prizes, experiencing synchronicity, or gaining a deeper understanding of astrology. Celebrating these successful moments keeps you energized and fosters a fullness of mind.

Practical tips and strategies to create personalized rituals and lottery practices that align with cosmic forces

1.   Surroundings of the sacred space:
Creating a sacred space for the lottery ceremony is essential to connect with the cosmic forces. Designate a special area where you can practice your lottery without interruption. Actively clean the room by applying sage, lighting incense sticks, or using crystals to purify the environment. Organize items of personal significance, such as statues, symbols, or amulets associated with good luck and abundance.

2.   Opening and closing ceremonies:
Begin your raffle ceremony by setting intentions and invoking the cosmic energy that will support your lottery efforts. This can be done through simple prayer, affirmation, or visualization by asking for advice and blessings from heaven. At the end of the ceremony, the cosmic help received is appreciated, and the ceremony ends with the bursting of candles or the performance of symbolic gestures such as applause or bells to signal the completion of the sacred space.

3.   Affirmations and mantras:
Incorporate affirmations and mantras into your lottery ritual to reinforce positive beliefs and focus your energy on the desired outcome. Create personalized statements that align with your intentions, such as "I'm a magnet for lottery prizes," "I rely on

cosmic forces to guide me to the right opportunities," or "I'm ready to accept the abundance of the universe." Repeat these affirmations or mantras in your ritual to allow your vibrations to penetrate your presence and create a strong resonance with cosmic forces.

4.   Visualization and presentation:

Harness the power of visualization and representation in your raffle ceremony.

Close your eyes and imagine holding your winning ticket and experiencing the joy and excitement of claiming your prize. Imagine the money flowing through your life and allow yourself to experience the emotions associated with financial abundance. Keep this image in your head and inject positive energy and intention into it. It is believed that the universe is working hard to turn this vision into reality.

5.   Symbolic actions and products:

Incorporate symbolic acts and offerings into your lottery ceremony to deepen your connection to the cosmic forces. This may involve lighting candles, placing crystals or gemstones associated with good luck and abundance on the altar, or making small signs of gratitude to the universe. These symbolic gestures can serve as a physical representation of your intentions and act as a catalyst to achieve the desired result.

6.   Alignment of the Moon:

Use the phases and lunar cycles as a backdrop for the raffle ceremony. Align your practice with the New Moon to set intentions and start a new lottery. Use the full moon to let go of doubts, fears, or limiting beliefs that could hinder your success. Adapt your rituals and practices during the lunar month to the rising and descending energies of the moon. By consciously adapting to the lunar cycle, you can synchronize your lottery efforts with the natural rhythms of the universe.

7.   Numerological meaning:

Incorporate numerological meaning into your lottery rituals and practices to strengthen your connection to the cosmic forces. Discover the numerological oscillations related to your date of birth, lucky numbers or important dates related to your participation in the lottery. Incorporate these numbers into your ritual by lighting the appropriate number of candles, arranging objects in a numbering pattern, or reciting certain mantras or statements that are consistent with numerological energy. By imbuing your ritual with numerological meaning, you strengthen the energetic resonance between you and the forces of the universe.

8.   Cosmic offers:

Consider making offerings to cosmic forces to acknowledge and invoke their help in lottery efforts. Offerings can take many forms, such as lighting candles or incense sticks as a symbol of devotion, placing flowers or herbs on an altar as a sign of gratitude, or even performing acts of kindness and generosity according to the principle of abundance. These offerings are tangible expressions of your commitment and respect for the energy of the universe.

9.   Diary notes and reflections:

Incorporate journaling and reflection into your lottery rituals and practices. Before and after the ceremony, take the time to write down your intentions, experiences, and intuitive ideas that come your way. Use your journal as a sacred place to record your progress, record synchronicity, and track consistency between astrological influences and lottery results. Regularly review your diary entries for insights and refine your strategy based on your observations.

10.   Develop patience and self-confidence:

While rituals and practices can strengthen your connection with cosmic forces, it is important to develop patience and confidence in performing sacred time. Avoid sticking to specific deliverables or deadlines, and instead focus on maintaining a sense of trust and delivery. To understand that cosmic forces work in mysterious ways, perfect alignment takes time. Embrace the journey and be open to unexpected opportunities and blessings that may arise along the way.

III. Balance optimism with realistic expectations for a satisfying lottery experience.

1. Practical advice and strategies: Balance optimism with realistic expectations for a satisfying lottery experience

At the end of our journey through the fascinating world of astrology and its application to the prediction lottery, it is important to grapple with the importance of balancing optimism and realistic expectations.

While astrology provides valuable information and tools to increase our chances of success in the lottery, the lottery should be approached with a solid perspective that acknowledges the reality of the game.

2. Harness the power of positive thinking:

Optimism plays an important role in achieving positive results.

Develop a positive, optimistic attitude when participating in the lottery.

Believe in your ability to attract the rich and imagine that you are a winner.

By aligning your thoughts and emotions with positive expectations, you can create fertile ground to achieve positive results.

3. Set realistic goals:

It's important to dream big, but it's equally important to set realistic goals.

Set your lottery goals based on your situation and the odds associated with winning.

Consider factors such as the size of the jackpot, the odds of winning, and the number of times you participate in the lottery.

By setting realistic goals, you can maintain a balanced

perspective and avoid unrealistic expectations that can lead to disappointment.

4.   Understand the probabilities:
Know the odds of winning more lottery games.
Each game has different odds of winning, and knowing them will help you make an informed decision. Considering that winning the lottery is a statistical challenge, the probability of winning is usually low.
However, this does not mean that this is impossible.
Knowing the odds will allow you to approach the game with a realistic mindset while maintaining hope of success.

5.   Manage your budget:
Participation in the lottery should always be done within its limits.
Set a specific budget for the lottery and stick to it.
Avoid overspending or being financially stressed when looking for a jackpot.
By managing your budget responsibly, you can enjoy the thrill of the lottery without putting your finances at risk.

6.   Diversify your strategy:
Instead of relying solely on the lottery to achieve financial sufficiency, consider diversifying your wealth creation strategy.
Explore other options, such as investing, starting a business, or looking for other sources of income.
This broader approach ensures multiple opportunities for financial growth and success.

7.   Celebrate small victories:
While the goal is to win the jackpot, you shouldn't overlook the value of the small winners.
Celebrate any small rewards or positive experiences you encounter along the way. Whether you're guessing a few numbers or experiencing timing based on your lottery predictions, recognize and cherish these moments as a sign of progress.

Celebrating small successes can motivate you and help you stay positive.

8.   Focus on the experience:

Stop focusing on the winning outcome of the lottery, but enjoy the overall experience.

Take part in the raffle with a sense of fun, excitement and anticipation.

The thrill of seizing the opportunity and the joy of participating.

By focusing on the journey and not just the destination, you can be satisfied with the process itself.

9.   Practice gratitude:

Be grateful for the opportunities and experiences you find, whether you win or not.

Develop an attitude that appreciates the wealth that already exists in your life. Gratitude will raise your vibration and allow you to attract more positive experiences.

Realize that even if you don't hit the jackpot, you're lucky in many ways.

10.   Belief in the Holy Time:

Belief in the sacred time of the universe.

To understand that cosmic forces work in mysterious ways, the best time to succeed in the lottery may not meet your immediate expectations.

Trust that the universe has a plan for you and that everything will happen at the right time. Patience and trust are the basic virtues of lottery and astrology.

Be open to unexpected opportunities and blessings that may arise, even if they don't meet your initial expectations.

11.   In search of personal growth:

See your participation in the lottery as an opportunity for personal growth and self-discovery.

Self-reflection and introspection throughout the trip.

Discover your lessons, ideas and experiences by entering the raffle. Use this process as a catalyst for personal development and as a springboard for improvements in other areas of your life.

12.   A balanced point of view:
Strive for a balanced perspective that recognizes both the potential for success and the reality of the possibilities.
While optimism is essential, it must be reconciled with great realism. Avoid being too obsessed with winning the lottery and remember that this is only one aspect of a full and rich life.
With a balanced perspective, you can enjoy the lottery experience without being consumed by it.

CHAPTER 14.
BALANCING OPTIMISM AND REALISM:

Anticipation is the key to a rewarding lottery experience.

By embracing the power of positive thinking, setting realistic goals, understanding odds, managing budgets, diversifying strategies, celebrating small winners, focusing on experiences, practicing gratitude, believing in sacred time, striving for personal growth, and maintaining a balanced perspective, you can approach the lottery with a healthy mindset.

Astrology provides valuable information and tools to increase the chances of success, but it is important to remember that the lottery is a game of chance.
Enjoy the process, open yourself to possibilities, and trust the cosmic forces that drive your journey.
By balancing optimism and reality, you can create a rewarding and rewarding lottery experience regardless of the outcome.

Remember that the true measure of abundance is not only winning the lottery, but also the growth, gratitude, and joy you cultivate along the way.
As mentioned above, let your lottery journey be filled with positivity, wisdom, and achievement as follows.

Immerse yourself in the fascinating world of astrological lottery predictions:

Astrology adds an exciting and rich dimension to the lottery.
By understanding the effects of heaven and aligning your actions with cosmic energy, you can maximize your chances of success.
However, it is important to treat participation in the lottery responsibly.
Responsible gambling and personal financial management should always come first. Participation in the lottery must be within its possible limits and not cause financial difficulties.

Astrology can provide information and advice, but it cannot guarantee concrete results.
Whatever the outcome, it's important to maintain a balanced perspective, manage expectations, and enjoy the journey.
When embarking on an astrological lottery adventure, remember that the beauty of astrology lies in its flexibility and personal interpretation.
Each person has a unique birth chart and cosmic imprint that opens up endless possibilities for exploration.

Trust your instincts, try different techniques and adapt them to your preferences and environment.
Your experience and personal knowledge will deepen your understanding of astrology and its application to the lottery.

The most important thing is to make the process a source of joy, admiration and personal growth.
Participation in astrology as part of the lottery allows you to connect with cosmic forces, expand your consciousness and explore the mysteries of the universe.

It is an opportunity to explore the interaction between celestial bodies and the earthly world, where the boundaries between the everyday and the magical are blurred.

Discover Your Astrological Lottery Journey:

In this book, we begin our fascinating exploration of astrology and its application in predictive lotteries.

We delve into the complex connections between the celestial realm and the earthly realm, discovering the power of astrological signs, houses, planetary patterns, time technology, moon phases, ascending signs, and more.

To conclude this enlightening journey, I encourage readers to further explore and expand their understanding of astrology in the context of the lottery.

Astrology is a vast and evolving field full of infinite possibilities for exploration and interpretation.

While we've covered a wide range of topics and provided practical advice and strategies, it's important to remember that there's always more to learn and discover.

Each person has a unique astrological horoscope and a cosmic level that opens the door to infinite perception and connection.

Take the opportunity to dive deeper into your birth chart, study planetary influences, and observe patterns that emerge from your lottery experience.

Continuing your astrological lottery journey will keep you open-minded and curious.

Explore different techniques, try different strategies, and adapt them to your individual needs and preferences.

Trust your instincts and develop your own personalized approach to using astrology to predict the lottery.

Let your understanding of astrology grow and evolve with each new experience as you discover deeper wisdom and meaning.

However, it is crucial to maintain a balanced perspective when embarking on this journey.

While astrology adds an intriguing dimension to the lottery, it's important to remember that winning the lottery is ultimately a matter of chance.

Astrology can provide information and advice, but it does not guarantee concrete results. Responsible gambling and personal

financial management should always come first.
Set realistic expectations, manage budgets, and treat the lottery with fun and curiosity without just focusing on the results.

Finally, remember that astrology isn't just about predicting lottery outcomes.
It is a powerful tool for self-discovery, personal growth, and understanding of the cosmic forces at work in life.
Use astrology to deepen your connection to the universe, better understand its strengths and challenges, and navigate the ebb and flow of life with greater awareness.
So, when you've finished reading the book and embark on your astrological lottery journey, take advantage of the opportunities that astrology offers. Explore, experience and trust the wisdom of the heavenly energy.
Let astrology enrich your lottery experience and gain a deeper understanding of the interrelationships of the universe.
May your journey be full of wonder, self-discovery and a deep connection with the cosmic dance of the stars.
As mentioned above, you may find harmony and satisfaction in the astrological lottery as follows.

Adopt astrology if you participate responsibly in the lottery:

To conclude this fascinating journey of astrology and its application to lottery prediction, it is important to emphasize the importance of responsible gambling and personal financial management.
While astrology undoubtedly adds an exciting dimension to participating in the lottery, it should always be managed responsibly and financially.

Astrology provides valuable information and tools to enhance your lottery experience, increase your chances of success, and deepen your connection to cosmic energy.
It provides a fascinating lens through which we can understand

the interaction between the celestial forces and our earthly existence. But

It is important to remember that astrology does not guarantee certain results.

Participating in the lottery is essentially a game of chance and winning is never inevitable.

Responsible gaming should always be a priority.
Set a budget for your participation in the lottery and stick to it.
Don't spend more than you can afford to lose.
The lottery is meant to be fun, and while winning is undoubtedly exciting, it should never come at the expense of your financial stability and well-being.

Equally important is the management of personal finances.
Don't just rely on the lottery as a means of financial salvation or immediate wealth.
It's important to diversify your financial strategy, explore other ways of wealth creation, and take a long-term approach to strengthening your financial security.
Use astrology as a complementary tool, as well as responsible financial planning, investing, and other forms of income generation.
Remember that astrology is not a substitute for common sense, discipline and hard work.

It should be seen as a supportive guide that includes ideas and recommendations, but the final decision and action is up to you.
Use astrology as inspiration, advice and self-reflection.
This can help you align your intentions with cosmic energy and make informed decisions, but it cannot replace personal action and responsibility.

Approach the lottery with a balanced mindset. Enjoy the thrill of participating, the opportunities it offers, and the experiences that take place along the way.
Celebrate every victory, no matter how small, and enjoy the

moments of joy and excitement that arise.
Keep in mind that the value of the lottery experience goes beyond the results themselves.

It's an opportunity for personal growth, self-discovery, and building resilience.
While astrology adds an exciting dimension to lottery participation, responsible gambling and managing personal finances should always be a priority.
Use astrology as a tool to enhance your lottery experience, deepen your connection with cosmic forces, and better understand your unique journey.
Combine this with responsible decision-making, rigorous budgeting, and long-term financial planning to ensure a balanced and satisfying approach to the lottery.

As mentioned above, let your lottery activities be filled with wisdom, responsibility, and a deep connection to the cosmic energies that shape our lives as follows.
Use astrology as a guiding star, but always remember that you have the power to create destiny.

Inference

Let your imagination run wild, trust the alignment of the universe and embark on an exciting journey with the astrological prediction lottery.

Whether you win the jackpot or not, the exploration itself will be a rewarding and rewarding experience.
Remember that the stars have a story to tell, and astrology provides a roadmap to decipher your message.
Accept the possibilities, open your heart to the wisdom of the universe and let yourself be guided by the cosmic dance.
Good luck and may star formation be in your favor!

www.ingramcontent.com/pod-product-compliance
Lightning Source LLC
Chambersburg PA
CBHW070855260726
48661CB00004B/1428